Ninja Foodi 2-Basket Air Fryer Cookbook for Beginners UK 2023

365 day Simple, Affordable, and Delicious Recipes for your family using dual zone air fryer.

Kamani Rodger

© **Copyright 2023 Kamani Rodger - All Rights Reserved.**

It is in no way legal to reproduce, duplicate, or transmit any part of this document by either electronic means or in printed format. Recording of this publication is strictly prohibited, and any storage of this material is not allowed unless with written permission from the publisher. All rights reserved.

The information provided herein is stated to be truthful and consistent, in that any liability, regarding inattention or otherwise, by any usage or abuse of any policies, processes, or directions contained within is the solitary and complete responsibility of the recipient reader. Under no circumstances will any legal liability or blame be held against the publisher for any reparation, damages, or monetary loss due to the information herein, either directly or indirectly.

Respective authors own all copyrights not held by the publisher.

Legal Notice:

This book is copyright protected. This is only for personal use. You cannot amend, distribute, sell, use, quote or paraphrase any part of the content within this book without the consent of the author or copyright owner. Legal action will be pursued if this is breached.

Disclaimer Notice:

Please note the information contained within this document is for educational and entertainment purposes only. Every attempt has been made to provide accurate, up-to-date, reliable, and complete information. No warranties of any kind are expressed or implied. Readers acknowledge that the author is not engaging in the rendering of legal, financial, medical or professional advice.

By reading this document, the reader agrees that under no circumstances are we responsible for any losses, direct or indirect, which are incurred as a result of the use of information contained within this document, including, but not limited to, errors, omissions, or inaccuracies.

Table of Contents

Introduction 5

Chapter 1: Breakfast 11

Chapter 2: Vegetables..22

Chapter 3: Meats 33

Chapter 4: Poultry 45

Chapter 5: Casseroles, Frittatas, and Quiches 56

Chapter 6: Desserts 62

Chapter 7: Wraps and Sandwiches 79

Chapter 8: Appetizers and Snacks.................85

Chapter 9: Sauces, Dips, and Dressings 97

Conclusion.. 103

Appendix recipe Index................................... 104

INTRODUCTION

Welcome to the wonderful world of air frying in the United Kingdom! Air fryers have become a popular kitchen appliance in recent years, and it's no wonder why. With an air fryer, you can enjoy delicious and healthy meals with less oil and less mess than traditional frying methods.

This cookbook will guide you through the basics of air frying, including how to choose the right air fryer for your needs, how to use it safely, and how to clean it properly. You'll also find a wide variety of recipes to suit every taste, from classic British favorites like fish and chips to international dishes like Chinese stir fry.

In addition to main dishes, you'll also find recipes for sides, snacks, and desserts that you can make in your air fryer. And because air frying is so easy and convenient, you'll find yourself using it more and more often in your daily cooking routine.

So whether you're new to air frying or an experienced user, this cookbook is sure to become a valuable resource in your kitchen. Happy air frying!

An Overview of Air Fryer

An air fryer is a kitchen appliance that uses hot air to cook food. It's essentially a small convection oven that circulates hot air around the food to create a crispy exterior and tender interior, without the need for deep frying in oil.

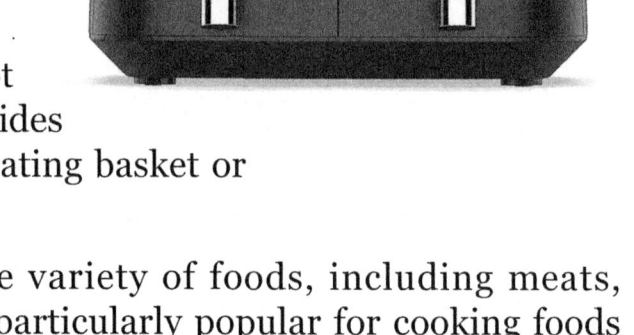

Air fryers typically have a basket or tray to hold the food, which is placed in the cooking chamber. A fan circulates hot air around the food, cooking it from all sides at once. Some air fryers also have a rotating basket or other features to ensure even cooking.

Air fryers can be used to cook a wide variety of foods, including meats, vegetables, and even desserts. They're particularly popular for cooking foods that are traditionally deep-fried, such as French fries, chicken wings, and onion rings, as they can produce a crispy, crunchy texture without the added oil and mess of deep frying.

One of the main benefits of using an air fryer is that it can cook food quickly and efficiently. It can also be a healthier cooking option than traditional deep frying, as it can use up to 80% less oil to achieve similar results.

Overall, air fryers are a versatile and convenient appliance that can help you cook a wide variety of foods quickly and easily, while also offering a healthier alternative to traditional frying methods.

How Does An Air Fryer Work?

An air fryer works by circulating hot air around the food to cook it. The appliance typically consists of a cooking chamber, a heating element, and a fan.

When you turn on the air fryer, the heating element heats the air inside the cooking chamber to a high temperature.

The fan then circulates this hot air around the food, cooking it from all sides at once.

As the hot air circulates around the food, it creates a crispy exterior, similar to deep frying, but with much less oil. This is because the hot air helps to evaporate the moisture on the food's surface, creating a crispy texture.

Air fryers can also be used to cook a variety of foods, from meats and vegetables to frozen foods and even desserts. They offer a quick and easy way to cook food without using excess oil, making them a popular alternative to traditional frying methods.

Overall, air fryers are a convenient and efficient way to cook food, providing a healthier and less messy option than deep frying.

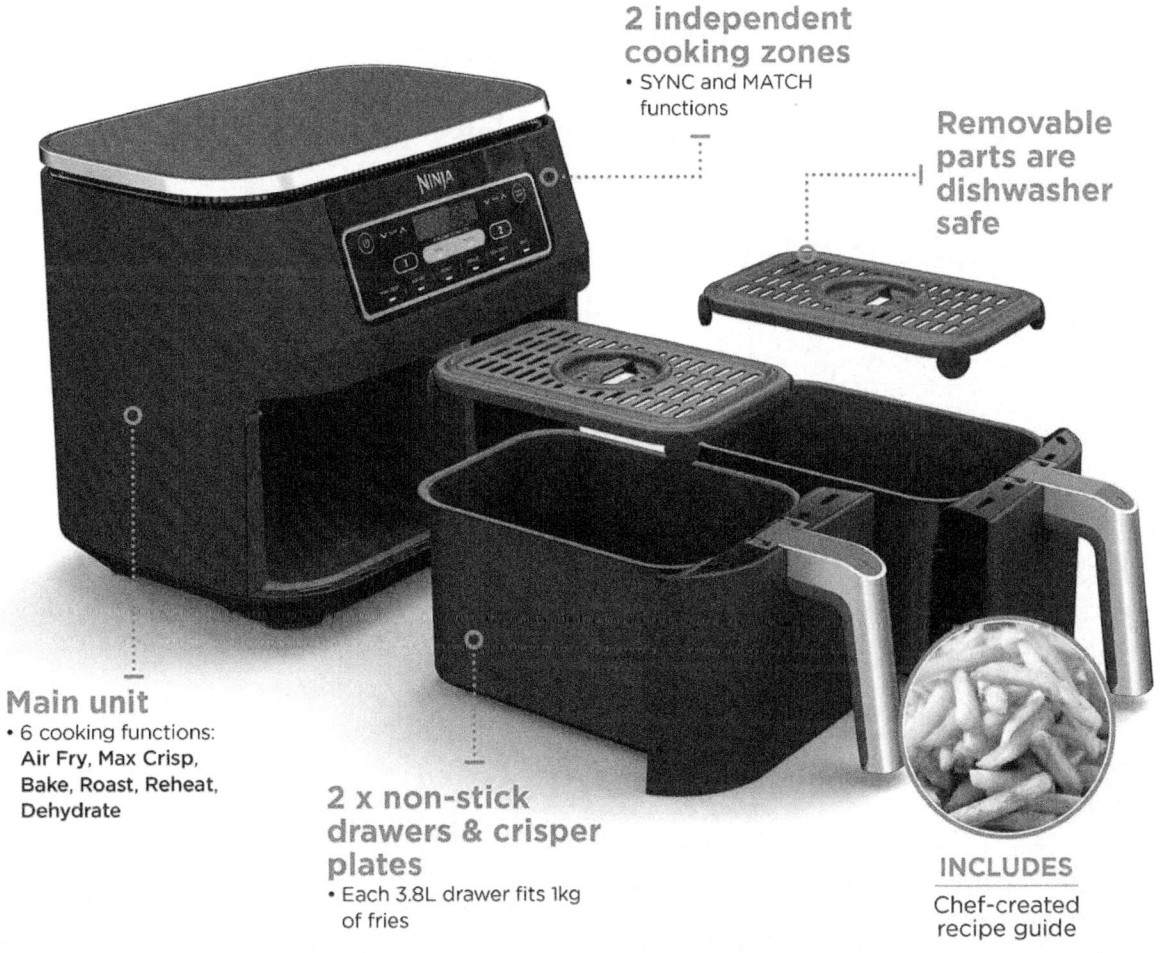

Parts & Functions Of An Air Fryer

An air fryer typically consists of several parts and functions that work together to cook food quickly and efficiently. Here are the main parts and functions of an air fryer:

- Cooking Chamber: This is the main area where the food is placed for cooking. It is usually a non-stick basket or tray that can be easily removed for cleaning.

- Heating Element: This is the part that heats the air inside the cooking chamber. It is usually located at the top of the appliance.

- Fan: The fan is responsible for circulating the hot air around the food, ensuring even cooking.

- Control Panel: This is where you can adjust the temperature and cooking time, as well as select pre-programmed cooking modes for specific types of food.

- Air Inlet: This is where air enters the air fryer and is heated by the heating element.

- Exhaust Vent: This is where the hot air exits the air fryer, helping to regulate the temperature inside the cooking chamber.

- Power Cord: This is how the air fryer is connected to an electrical outlet.

The functions of an air fryer can vary depending on the model, but typically include temperature control, cooking time control, pre-programmed cooking modes, and automatic shut-off. Some air fryers may also have additional functions such as rotisserie cooking or baking.as Greece, Italy, and Spain. The diet emphasizes a plant-based, whole foods approach to eating, with an em

Health Benefits Of Air Frying

Air frying offers several potential health benefits over traditional deep-frying methods. Here are some of the main health benefits of air frying:• Fruits: apples, oranges, berries, bananas, grapes, pears, peaches, and more.

- Lower Fat Content: Air frying requires much less oil than traditional deep frying, which can reduce the overall fat content of your food. This can be particularly beneficial if you're trying to manage your weight or reduce your intake of unhealthy fats.

- Reduced Calorie Intake: By reducing the amount of oil used in cooking, air frying can also help reduce the overall calorie content of your meals. This can be particularly helpful if you're trying to lose weight or maintain a healthy weight.

- Less Exposure to Harmful Compounds: Deep frying can produce harmful compounds such as acrylamide, which has been linked to an increased risk of cancer. Air frying reduces the formation of these compounds, which can help lower your risk of health problems.

- Healthier Food Choices: Air frying can make it easier to choose healthier food options, as it can be used to cook a wide variety of foods without the added fat and calories of traditional frying methods.

- Quick and Easy Cooking: Air frying can be a convenient and time-saving cooking method, as it can cook food quickly and with minimal prep time.

This can make it easier to prepare healthy meals at home, rather than relying on takeout or fast food.

Overall, air frying can offer several potential health benefits, particularly if you're looking to reduce your intake of unhealthy fats and calories, and make healthier food choices.

MAX CRISP
Super fast air-flow circulates temperatures of 240°C to evenly cook and crisp food from frozen in minutes.

Crucial Tips For Air Frying Success

Air frying can be a convenient and healthy way to cook food, but there are a few tips you should keep in mind to ensure success. Here are some crucial tips for air frying:

- Preheat the Air Fryer: Preheating the air fryer can help ensure even cooking and a crispy texture. Most air fryers require only a few minutes to preheat.

- Don't Overcrowd the Basket: Overcrowding the basket can reduce air flow and result in uneven cooking. It's best to cook food in small batches to ensure even cooking.

- Use a Little Oil: While air frying requires less oil than traditional frying methods, adding a little oil to your food can help improve the texture and prevent sticking. It's best to use a high smoke point oil like avocado or canola oil.

- Shake the Basket: Shaking the basket or tray during cooking can help ensure even cooking and prevent sticking.

- Use the Right Temperature and Cooking Time: The right temperature and cooking time can vary depending on the type of food you're cooking. It's important to follow the instructions for your specific air fryer and adjust cooking times as needed based on your personal preferences.

- Use a Food Thermometer: To ensure that meat is cooked to a safe temperature, use a food thermometer to check the internal temperature.

- Clean the Air Fryer Regularly: Regular cleaning of the air fryer can help prevent buildup of grease and food residue, ensuring that it works properly and produces the best results.

By following these tips, you can help ensure that your air frying experience is a success, producing healthy and delicious food every time.

Chapter 1: Breakfast

Crispy Air Fryer Cauliflower

Prep Time: 5 Mins
Cook Time: 24 Mins
Serves: 4

Ingredients:

- 3-4 tbsp hot sauce please go for mild sauce if you don't like it hot
- 1 tbsp avocado oil
- Salt to taste
- 1 medium head of cauliflower cut into bites washed and fully patted dry

Directions:

1. Preheat air fryer to 200°C.
2. Mix together hot sauce, almond flour, avocado oil and salt in a large bowl.
3. Add the cauliflower and mix until coated.
4. Add half the cauliflower into the air fryer and fry for 12-15 min (or until crisp at the edges with a little bite still, or it reaches your desired doneness).
5. Make sure to open the air fryer and shake the frying basket 2-3 times to turn the cauliflower. Remove and set aside.
6. Add in second batch, but cook it for 2-3 mins less.
7. Serve warm (although they can also be served cold) with some extra hot sauce for dipping.

Nutritional Value (Amount per Serving):

Calories: 49; Fat: 3.69; Carb: 3.61; Protein: 1.34

Air Fried Beef Sausage Rolls

Prep Time: 5 Mins
Cook Time: 10 Mins
Serves: 2

Ingredients:

- 1 packet frozen puff pastry
- 8 Beef sausage I used

Directions:

1. I rolled out the packet (kilo).
2. Took the skins of a packet of 8 beef sausages.
3. Roll the sausage meat in some flour.put the onto the pastry and rolled pastry over the sausage and cut along the edge. I did this until I'd used all the pastry and sausages. I sprayed the crisping plate on my ninja and put sausage rolls all over. Brushed them with milk and cooked on air-fry 190 for 5 mins. then checked they were not burnt and put them on for another 5 mins.

Nutritional Value (Amount per Serving):

Calories: 277; Fat: 21.37; Carb: 12.26; Protein: 8.44

Air Fryer Pizza Scrolls

Prep Time: 10 Mins
Cook Time: 7 Mins
Serves: 6

Ingredients:

- 1/2 portion of pizza dough see my recipe linked above
- 2 portions of roasted tomato pizza sauce see my recipe linked above
- 60 g grated mozzarella and cheddar mix
- Mixed Italian herbs basil and oregano

Directions:

1. Roll out the pizza dough as thin as possible.
2. Spread over the tomato pizza sauce.
3. Add the grated cheddar.
4. Sprinkle on 1/2 of your herbs.
5. Roll up as tightly as possible. I find that using baking paper or cling film works well here.
6. Slice into 2.5cm slices.
7. Pop into the air fryer basket.
8. Bake at 200°C for 6-7 minutes until golden brown.
9. Sprinkle over the remainder of the herbs when serving.

Nutritional Value (Amount per Serving):

Calories: 324; Fat: 11.27; Carb: 42.2; Protein: 9.79

Corn Ribs Air Fryer

Prep Time: 10 Mins
Cook Time: 8 Mins
Serves: 8

Ingredients:

- 4 ears corn husked and cut into 16 ribs
- (15g) fresh parsley finely chopped
- (250g) mayonnaise
- ½ tablespoon ground chili
- 2 jalapeños optional, for serving
- (250g) cream cheese
- ½ tablespoon garlic powder
- ½ tablespoon Tabasco sauce
- 1 lime for serving

Directions:

1. Shuck the corn and cut off the ends. Rinse the corn to clean, then use a sharp knife to cut the corn vertically into quarters, creating four ribs from each ear of corn.
2. In a small bowl, combine the cream cheese, garlic powder, and parsley, mixing well to combine.
3. Brush cream cheese mixture onto the corn ribs with a silicone brush or spoon. Smooth the cream cheese mix on all sides. Make sure to leave as a thin layer so that the cheese doesn't burn.
4. Preheat air fryer to 200 degrees C for about 5 minutes.
5. Place the corn ribs into the air fryer basket and cook for 8 minutes, or until curled and lightly charred and crisp. Flip the corn ribs over after 4 minutes.
6. While corn is cooking, combine mayonnaise, ground chili, and Tabasco sauce in a small bowl.
7. Drizzle the corn ribs with spicy mayo before serving. Garnish with diced jalapenos and a squeeze of lime juice, and serve with lime wedges if desired.

Nutritional Value (Amount per Serving):

Calories: 312; Fat: 15.59; Carb: 16.46; Protein: 29.48

Air Fryer Peeps Rolls

Prep Time: 8 Mins
Cook Time: 10 Mins
Serves: 5

Ingredients:

- 1 tube store-bought flaky biscuits dough
- 5 Peeps Marshmallow Candies
- 70g Nutella chocolate hazelnut spread

Directions:

1. Preheat Air Fryer to 150 degrees C and lightly spray the air fryer basket.
2. Take 5 pieces of dough and pat them flat.
3. Place a Peeps marshmallow in the center of each piece of dough, then spoon a little Nutella spread on top of the Peeps.
4. Pat the other 5 pieces of dough float, and place on top of each of the Peeps. Pinch the sides closed, then roll into a ball.
5. Place each Peeps roll inside the air fryer basket and air fry for 10 minutes, or until cooked and golden brown.

Nutritional Value (Amount per Serving):

Calories: 268; Fat: 5.41; Carb: 54.36; Protein: 2.35

Air Fryer Vegan Fried Rice With Quorn Vegan Fillets

Prep Time: 10 Mins
Cook Time: 20 Mins
Serves: 2

Ingredients:

- 2 Quorn Vegan Fillets, defrosted and sliced
- 325g cold cooked rice
- 5 tbsp soy sauce
- 225g frozen vegetables (we used frozen edamame, peas, carrots and sweetcorn)
- 100g firm tofu, crumbled (optional)
- 1 tsp sesame oil
- 1 tsp vegetable oil
- 2 green spring onions, chopped
- Salt to taste

Directions:

1. Place cold rice into a large bowl, combine with frozen vegetables, tofu (if using) and Quorn Vegan Fillets and mix.
2. Add the soy sauce and oil to the bowl. Mix until well combined.
3. Line one zone of your Ninja Foodi Dual Zone Air Fryer with baking paper, pour in the rice ingredients, select air fry, set temperature to 180°C and set time to 15 minutes. Start/Stop your air fryer three times throughout the cooking time to stir.
4. Remove rice from the air fryer and sprinkle over chopped spring onions.

Nutritional Value (Amount per Serving):

Calories: 597; Fat: 33.02; Carb: 43.92; Protein: 32.58

Air Fryer Empanadas

Prep Time: 15 Mins
Cook Time: 10 Mins
Serves: 8

Ingredients:

- 1 ½ tablespoons olive oil
- 1 bell pepper deseeded and finely diced
- 1 white onion peeled and diced
- (450g) ground beef
- 2 garlic cloves minced
- 1 teaspoon oregano
- 1 teaspoon cumin
- ½ teaspoon ground paprika
- ¼ teaspoon ground cinnamon
- salt to taste
- 4 pitted green olives finely chopped
- 2-3 sheets pie crust dough
- 1 egg beaten

Directions:

1. Heat olive oil in a large skillet over medium heat. Sauté the onion and pepper until it becomes translucent and begins to soften.
2. Add ground beef and garlic and cook for about 5 minutes until beef is brown. Drain any excess fat.
3. Stir in the oregano, paprika, cinnamon, salt and olives and cook for a couple of minutes before letting the mixture cool.
4. Roll out pie crust and use a cookie or biscuit cutter to make 5-inch discs of dough.
5. Place 2 tablespoons of empanada mix into each disk of pie crust dough, being careful not to overfill.
6. Wet the edges of the pie crust with water, fold over to seal and crimp with a fork.

7. Brush the empanadas with egg wash.
8. Preheat an air fryer to 180 degrees C.
9. Spray empanadas with olive oil or cooking spray and place them in a single layer inside the air fryer basket.
10. Air fry for 8-10 minutes until golden, turning halfway through.

Nutritional Value (Amount per Serving):

Calories: 350; Fat: 22.01; Carb: 30.57; Protein: 7.77

Fried Oranges

Prep Time: 3 Mins
Cook Time: 8 Mins
Serves: 2

Ingredients:

- 2 medium navel oranges
- 1 tablespoon honey or maple syrup
- ½ teaspoon ground cinnamon

Directions:

1. Slice the oranges in half.
2. Add the honey and ground cinnamon in a small bowl. Stir to combine.
3. Brush the honey mixture onto the oranges. You may not need all of the honey, but you can save it to drizzle on later.
4. Place the oranges in the air fryer basket with the flesh facing up.
5. Air fry at 200°C for 5-8 minutes, until the oranges are starting to brown and the flesh is hot.
6. Serve immediately.

Nutritional Value (Amount per Serving):

Calories: 41; Fat: 0.06; Carb: 10.78; Protein: 0.29

Bacon Wrapped Dates Air Fryer

Prep Time: 10 Mins
Cook Time: 10 Mins
Serves: 6

Ingredients:

- 12 dates pitted
- 60g goat cheese
- 6 slices thin cut bacon
- 12 toothpicks

Directions:

1. Preheat air fryer to 200 degrees C.
2. Stuff dates with goat cheese and pinch the ends slightly to close them.
3. Cut the bacon strips in half lengthwise and wrap half a bacon slice around each of the stuffed dates, then secure with a toothpick. Continue until all are done.
4. Place dates in the air fryer basket and air fry for 10 minutes, carefully turning over halfway through cook time.
5. If bacon is not crisp enough, then continue cooking for a couple of minutes.

Nutritional Value (Amount per Serving):

Calories: 191; Fat: 13.82; Carb: 11.09; Protein: 6.66

Air Fryer Veggie Burgers

Prep Time: 5 Mins
Cook Time: 10 Mins
Serves: 4

Ingredients:

- 400g) white beans rinsed and drained (I used cannellini beans)
- 65g) oats
- 15g) fresh cilantro finely chopped
- 1/2 small onion grated or very finely diced
- 1/2 bell pepper, deseeded preferably grated or very finely diced
- juice of 1 lemon
- 3 Tablespoon sriracha sauce or tomato sauce
- 1 1/2 teaspoon Italian seasoning or oregano
- 1 teaspoon ground cumin
- 1/2 teaspoon smoked paprika
- 1/2 teaspoon garlic powder
- sea salt to taste

Directions:

1. Mash the beans in a mixing bowl.
2. Add in oats, cilantro, onion, bell pepper, lemon juice, sriracha sauce (or tomato sauce), herbs and spices and mix together.
3. Divide and shape into 4 patties.
4. Preheat Air Fryer to 180°C. Place patties in the basket, spray with olive oil or cooking spray and cook for 9-10 minutes flipping halfway through.
5. Create burgers with buns, patties and then desired toppings.

Nutritional Value (Amount per Serving):

Calories: 90; Fat: 1.88; Carb: 20.87; Protein: 4.82

Chapter 2: Vegetables

Air Fryer Eggplant

Prep Time: 5 Mins
Cook Time: 10 Mins
Serves: 4

Ingredients:

- 1 Large Eggplant (also known as Aubergine)
- ½ teaspoon Garlic
- ¼ teaspoon Black Pepper substitute with cayenne or chili flakes.
- ½ teaspoon Salt or to taste
- 1 teaspoon Paprika
- ¼ teaspoon Oregano
- 1 tablespoon Olive oil

Directions:

1. Preheat the air fryer to 180°C.
2. Wash the eggplant and cut it into fries, cubes, wedges. Whatever shape you chose, cut into equal size so they cook evenly.
3. Cut into fries.
4. Add into a bowl, then add in the paprika, garlic, oregano, pepper, salt (or any seasoning you've chosen), and olive oil. Mix well so they are well coated in the seasoning.
5. coated in seasoning
6. Arrange the eggplant in the air fryer basket in a single layer.
7. Air fry at a temperature of 180°C for 8 -10 minutes depending on the size you cut of eggplant.
8. Arranged in air fryer basket.
9. Bring out the basket and shake halfway through cooking so that all sides are cooked evenly.
10. The cooked dish in the air fryer basket.
11. When done, bring out the eggplant fries and serve.
12. It's best eaten warm. You can top with Garlic butter, Parmesan, cheese, or any topping of choice.

Nutritional Value (Amount per Serving):

Calories: 61; Fat: 4; Carb: 7; Protein: 1

Air Fryer Corn On The Cob

Prep Time: 2 Mins
Cook Time: 10 Mins
Serves: 3

Ingredients:

- 3 ears sweet corn
- Butter

Directions:

1. Prepare the corn by removing the husks and dividing each ear into thirds.
2. Rub each section with butter and place in air fryer tray. Set to air-fry at 200°C for 10 minutes
3. After 10 minutes it's ready! Super easy and tasty. Enjoy!

Nutritional Value (Amount per Serving):

Calories: 147; Fat: 4.26; Carb: 27.2; Protein: 4.76

Air Fryer Parsnip Fries

Cook Time: 17 Mins
Serves: 2

Ingredients:

- 3 Large Parsnips
- 1 Tbsp Extra Virgin Olive Oil
- 1 Tsp Basil
- 1 Tsp Parsley
- Salt & Pepper

Directions:

1. Peel your parsnips and chop the tops off them. Then cut them into 3rds. Then slice them into equal sized parsnip fries.
2. Load the parsnip fries into a bowl with the other ingredients and mix with your hands until the parsnips are well coated.
3. Load the parsnips into the air fryer basket and air fry your parsnips for 12 minutes at 160°C, shake and then air fry for a further 5 minutes at 180°C.
4. Serve your parsnip fries with ketchup, mayonnaise or your other favourite fries dipping sauce.

Nutritional Value (Amount per Serving):

Calories: 189; Fat: 3.75; Carb: 34.48; Protein: 3.15

Pulled Aubergine And Chickpea Curry

Prep Time: 10 Mins
Cook Time: 60 Mins
Serves: 4

Ingredients:

- 2 aubergines
- approximately 500g
- 3 tbsp oil
- 1 large onion, finely chopped
- 1 red pepper, diced
- 1 tbsp medium curry powder
- 1 tsp ground turmeric
- 2 tsp ground cumin
- 1 tsp garlic paste
- 1 tsp ginger paste
- 2 tbsp tomato puree,
- plus 3 tbsp water
- 1 x 400g can chopped

- tomatoes
- 300ml vegetable stock
- made with 1 low sodium
- vegetable stock cube
- 1 x 400g can chickpeas,
- drained and rinsed
- To serve
- 300g wholewheat basma ti
- rice, cooked as directed on
- the pack instructions
- Small bunch fresh
- coriander leaves

Directions:

1. Rub the aubergines with 1 tbsp oil and place on an air flow rack on the middle shelf of the air fryer. Set the temperature to 180°C and roast for 30 minutes, until the aubergines feel soft. Set aside to cool slightly.
2. Meanwhile, add onion, pepper and remaining oil to a 23cm square roasting tin and cook for 5 minutes at 180°C. Sprinkle over the dried spices, stir into the onion mixture and cook for a further minute.
3. Add the garlic, ginger paste, tomato puree and 3 tbsp water, then return the roasting tin to the air fryer and cook for a minute. Pour over the canned tomatoes and hot stock and increase the temperature to 200°C for 15 minutes.
4. Meanwhile, cut the aubergine in half and use a fork to pull out and shred the aubergine. Add the shredded aubergine and chickpeas to the curry and heat for 10 minutes, stirring halfway through.
5. Serve the rice in bowls with the curry alongside, garnished with coriander leaves.

Nutritional Value (Amount per Serving):

Calories: 1441; Fat: 109.65; Carb: 86.69; Protein: 39.5

Air Fryer Canned Potatoes

Prep Time: 2 Mins
Cook Time: 22 Mins
Serves: 2

Ingredients:

- 1 tin of canned potatoes – the ones I purchased were new baby potatoes in water 567g in volume, 345g once drained. Any similar quantity will be fine!
- Salt and pepper
- Vegetable spray oil
- Dried parsley
- Garlic powder
- Optional – paprika and rosemary

Directions:

1. Drain and rinse the potatoes. I like to rinse several times, just to remove any residue from the products they use to keep the potatoes fresh while canned.
2. Cut any larger potatoes in half or third as appropriate.
3. Then I dry them using a clean kitchen towel, but you can skip this step if you really want to save some effort.
4. Use a little spray oil on the potatoes.
5. Season with salt and pepper.
6. Cook at 180°C for 12 minutes.
7. Add 1/4 tsp of dried parsley, garlic powder and if you'd like then also add 1/4 tsp of paprika and rosemary.
8. Add a little more spray vegetable oil if needed.
9. Shake up.
10. Cook at 200°C for 10 minutes.
11. Serve and enjoy!

Nutritional Value (Amount per Serving):

Calories: 220; Fat: 16.11; Carb: 17.82; Protein: 7.47

Easy Air Fryer Baked Sweet Potatoes

Prep Time: 5 Mins
Cook Time: 30 Mins
Serves: 4

Ingredients:

- 4 sweet potatoes
- 1 teaspoon olive oil
- 1 pinch salt
- 1 pinch black pepper

Directions:

1. Wash the sweet potatoes and dry them well.
2. Prick all over with a fork or knife tip.
3. Rub with oil and season with salt and pepper.
4. Place in the air fryer on shelves or the basket of an air fryer, leaving a space between them.
5. Bake at 200°C for 30-35 minutes until soft.
6. Serve and enjoy!

Nutritional Value (Amount per Serving):

Calories: 18; Fat: 1.23; Carb: 1.87; Protein: 0.47

Air Fryer Sweet Potato Cubes

Prep Time: 5 Mins
Cook Time: 17 Mins
Serves: 2

Ingredients:

- 2 Large Sweet Potatoes
- 2 Tsp Extra Virgin Olive Oil
- 1 Tsp Parsley
- Salt & Pepper

Directions:

1. Peel and slice your sweet potatoes into chunks cubes, or roasted potatoes.
2. Load your sweet potatoes into a bowl with your seasonings and extra virgin olive oil and use your hands to thoroughly mix them.
3. Load the sweet potato cubes into the air fryer basket and cook for 12 minutes at 160°C.
4. Shake the air fryer basket, check with a fork that your potatoes are cooked and cook for a further 5 minutes at 200°C.
5. Serve and enjoy.

Nutritional Value (Amount per Serving):

Calories: 189; Fat: 2.29; Carb: 39.55; Protein: 3.99

Air Fryer Onions

Prep Time: 2 Mins
Cook Time: 14 Mins
Serves: 3

Ingredients:

- 1 white onion
- 1 tablespoon of vegetable oil
- 1/8 teaspoon of white sugar

Directions:

1. Chop off both ends of your onion and peel away the skin.
2. Cut the onion in half.
3. Slice each half into semi-circle shapes, around 1/2 cm thick.
4. Lightly dress the onions with your oil. Don't add the sugar yet.
5. Lay the onions in the air fryer basket, or underneath if you're cooking other items at the same time.
6. Cook at 150°C for 6 minutes, stirring halfway through.
7. Add the sugar and mix well to ensure all the onions have a little coating.
8. Cook at 150°C for another 8 minutes, stirring halfway through.
9. If you want grilled caramelised style onions then you can remove them now.
10. If you want very crispy onions then you can continue cooking for another 4-5 minutes, at 150°C, until they are super crispy.

Nutritional Value (Amount per Serving):

Calories: 55; Fat: 4.57; Carb: 3.52; Protein: 0.4

Air Fryer Aubergine

Prep Time: 5 Mins
Cook Time: 35 Mins
Serves: 4

Ingredients:

- 1 medium aubergine
- 1 tbsp. extra-virgin olive oil
- 1 tsp. dried oregano
- 1/2 tsp. garlic powder
- Salt
- Freshly ground black pepper
- Pinch chilli flakes

Directions:

1. Cut ends off of aubergine and cut in half lengthwise. Cut each half into strips about 2.5cm thick and 7cm long. In a medium bowl, add aubergine, oil, and seasonings and toss to coat.
2. Working in batches, arrange in basket of air fryer in a single layer. Cook at 190°C until golden, about 14 minutes, shaking the basket once about halfway through.

Nutritional Value (Amount per Serving):

Calories: 568; Fat: 33.55; Carb: 67.32; Protein: 5.06

Air Fryer Sliced Potatoes

Prep Time: 10 Mins
Cook Time: 15 Mins
Serves: 4

Ingredients:

- 500 g (1lb) Potatoes
- 1 teaspoon Paprika
- ½ teaspoon Garlic powder
- ½ teaspoon Onion granules
- ½ teaspoon Parsley
- ½ teaspoon Rosemary or Thyme
- ¼ teaspoon Black pepper or to taste
- Salt to taste
- 1 tablespoon Olive oil

Directions:

1. Peel the potatoes, wash them and pat dry with paper towels. If you prefer not to peel the potatoes, wash the potatoes thoroughly to remove any dirt on the skin then pat dry with kitchen towel.
2. Slice the potatoes into even slices.
3. Transfer the potatoes into a bowl then add in paprika, parsley, rosemary, onion granules, garlic powder, black pepper, salt and olive oil. Mix till all well combined.
4. Pour the potatoes into the air fryer basket and spread them out.
5. Air fry sliced potatoes at a temperature of 180°C for 8 minutes, bring out the basket shake it, and air fry potatoes for another 8 minutes or until the potatoes are tender inside and crispy outside.
6. Bring out the potatoes, and serve.

Nutritional Value (Amount per Serving):

Calories: 131; Fat: 4; Carb: 23; Protein: 3

Chapter 3: Meat

Air Fryer Sausages

Prep Time: 3 Mins
Cook Time: 10 Mins
Serves: 8

Ingredients:

- 8 sausages

Directions:

1. Preheat the air fryer to 180°C.
2. Pierce each sausage with a knife or fork.
3. Lay sausages in the air fryer basket.
4. Cook for 10 minutes, checking on them and turning them over after 5 minutes.

Nutritional Value (Amount per Serving):

Calories: 73; Fat: 5.15; Carb: 2.79; Protein: 5.25

Spicy Country Fries

Prep Time: 10 Mins
Cook Time: 20 Mins
Serves: 4

Ingredients:

- 800 g waxy potatoes
- 2 small, dried chilies or 1 heaped teaspoon freshly ground, dried chili flakes
- ½ tablespoon freshly ground black pepper
- 1 tablespoon olive oil

Directions:

1. Preheat the Air Fryer to 180°C.
2. Scrub the potatoes clean under running water. Cut them lengthwise into 1½ cm strips.
3. Soak the fries in water for at least 30 minutes. Drain them thoroughly and then pat them dry with kitchen paper.
4. Crush the chilies very finely (in a mortar) and mix them in a bowl with the olive oil, pepper and curry powder. Coat the fries with this mixture.
5. Transfer the fries to the fryer basket and slide the basket into the Air Fryer. Set the timer to 20 minutes and fry the fries until they are golden brown and done. Turn them every now and again.
6. Serve the fries in a platter and sprinkle with salt. Delicious with steak.

Nutritional Value (Amount per Serving):

Calories: 765; Fat: 44.19; Carb: 34.94; Protein: 54.3

Air Fryer Pork Chops

Prep Time: 5 Mins
Cook Time: 12 Mins
Serves: 1

Ingredients:

- 1 pork chop
- 1/2 tbsp olive oil
- 1/2 tbsp seasoning (see notes)

Directions:

1. Preheat the air fryer to 200°C.
2. Brush oil on each side of the pork chop.
3. Add seasoning and rub it in evenly all over.
4. Place pork chop in the preheated air fryer and set the timer for 12 minutes. Turn the pork chop over at around the 6 minute mark.
5. Check the pork chop is cooked all the way through - it should be golden brown on the outside and juices should run clear.

Nutritional Value (Amount per Serving):

Calories: 402; Fat: 24.16; Carb: 2.49; Protein: 40.4

Crispy Air Fryer Bacon

Prep Time: 5 Mins
Cook Time: 10 Mins
Serves: 8

Ingredients:

- 340 g thick-cut bacon

Directions:

1. Lay bacon inside air fryer basket in a single layer.
2. Set air fryer to 200°C and cook until crispy, about 10 minutes. (You can check halfway through and rearrange slices with tongs.)

Nutritional Value (Amount per Serving):

Calories: 132; Fat: 12.55; Carb: 2.69; Protein: 4.54

Bombay Potato Keema Pie

Prep Time: 10 Mins
Cook Time: 50 Mins
Serves: 4

Ingredients:

- 500g lean minced beef
- 1 medium onion, chopped
- 1 red pepper, diced
- 3 tbsp vegetable oil
- 2 tsp ground cumin
- 1 tsp garlic powder
- 3 tbsp tikka curry paste
- 3 tbsp tomato puree
- 325ml hot beef stock
- 1 tbsp cornflour mixed with
- 1 tbsp cold water
- 750g potatoes, peeled and
- chopped into 2cm dice
- 1 tsp turmeric
- 1 tsp nigella seeds
- 75g frozen peas, defrosted
- Salt and black pepper
- Small bunch coriander/
- 1 tbsp

Directions:

1. Put the minced beef, onion and pepper into a small roasting tin (approximately 23cm square) and drizzle over 1 tbsp oil. Break up the mince with a wooden spoon and mix everything together to coat in the oil. Put the tin on the middle shelf of the air fryer and set the temperature to 180°C for 10 minutes.

2. Sprinkle over the cumin and garlic powder, then stir in the tikka paste and cook for another 3 minutes at 180°C
3. Stir in the tomato puree, beef stock and cornflour, return the tin to the air fryer on the middle shelf and set the temperature to 190°C for 25 minutes, stirring a couple of times during the cooking time.
4. Meanwhile, bring a saucepan of water to the boil, add the potatoes and simmer for 8-10 minutes, until the potatoes are just tender. Drain in a colander, then return to the pan and toss with the turmeric, nigella seeds and remaining oil.
5. When the filling is cooked, stir in the peas, check the seasoning and transfer to a round pie dish (approximately 23cm by 5cm deep), arrange the potatoes on top and return the pie to the air fryer for 10 minutes, until the potatoes are crisp and golden. 6. Sprinkle over the coriander and serve.

Nutritional Value (Amount per Serving):

Calories: 657; Fat: 29.02; Carb: 47.96; Protein: 53.29

Air Fryer Thai Meatballs

Prep Time: 5 Mins
Cook Time: 10 Mins
Serves: 2

Ingredients:

- Soup Maker Lentil Soup
- 1 kg Minced Pork/Ground Pork
- ½ Medium Red Onion
- 1 Tbsp Philadelphia Light Herbs
- 2 Tsp Garlic Puree
- 1 Tbsp Thai 7 Spice Seasoning
- ½ Tsp Ground Ginger
- 5 Kaffir Lime Leaves
- Salt & Pepper

Directions:

1. Peel and thinly dice your red onion. Thinly slice your Thai leaves.
2. Load into a bowl all your meatball ingredients and mix with your hands for a well coating of the seasoning and the onion.
3. Make into Thai balls using the measuring scales to get equal sized meatballs. We did our meatballs to 47g each.
4. Do all meatballs and then cook them in batches to what will fit in your air fryer.
5. Load the Thai meatballs into the air fryer basket and air fry for 10 minutes at 180°C.
6. When the air fryer beeps serve your Thai meatballs over your lentil soup before serving.

Nutritional Value (Amount per Serving):

Calories: 1016; Fat: 68.58; Carb: 34.12; Protein: 67.87

Air Fryer Pork Roast

Prep Time: 10 Mins
Cook Time: 1 Hr 20 Mins
Serves: 4

Ingredients:

- 1.2 kg Pork Shoulder
- 1 kg Air Fryer Sweet Potato Cubes
- 1 Tbsp Olive Oil
- 1 Tbsp Parsley
- 1 tsp Garlic Powder
- Salt & Pepper

Directions:

1. Score your pork roast with similar sized square slits. Spray with extra virgin olive oil. Season your pork with salt and pepper and your other seasonings.
2. Place the rod through the pork shoulder so that it has come through both ends.
3. Secure the clamps on each side.
4. Place in the air fryer oven and make sure its secure. Set the time to 1 hour and the temperature to 180°C.
5. When the air fryer beeps, remove from the air fryer to rest.
6. After it has rested for about 5 minutes remove the clamps and rod and allow to rest for 5 minutes before slicing.

Nutritional Value (Amount per Serving):

Calories: 943; Fat: 57.77; Carb: 23.79; Protein: 81.76

Air Fryer Steak Bites

Prep Time: 5 Mins
Cook Time: 10 Mins
Serves: 4

Ingredients:

- 500 g Steak Rib eye, Sirloin, or any good cut.
- 1 teaspoon Garlic Powder
- ½ teaspoon Ginger powder
- ½ teaspoon Dried Parsley
- ½ teaspoon Black pepper or to taste
- Salt to taste
- 1 tablespoon Olive oil
- or Garlic Butter
- 2 tablespoons Butter
- 1 teaspoon Garlic minced
- 1 tablespoon Fresh Parsley finely chopped

Directions:

1. First, make the garlic herb butter by mixing the butter, garlic, and parsley together. Wrap in baking paper, or clingfilm, and put it in the fridge to chill.
2. Next, cut the steak into cube bite size.
3. Add the garlic powder, black pepper, ginger, salt, parsley, and oil to the steak cuts and mix till well combined.
4. Arrange the steak bites in the air fryer basket in a single layer without overlapping.
5. Air fry at 190°C for 4-5 minutes. Flip the steak bites using a tong (or shake) then continue to air fry it for another 4-5 minutes.
6. Take the steak bites out of the air fryer and immediately add the garlic butter to it.
7. Serve and enjoy as a snack or with any side of choice for a complete meal.

Nutritional Value (Amount per Serving):

Calories: 293; Fat: 21; Carb: 1; Protein: 25

My Air Fryer Honey Mustard Pork Balls

Prep Time: 5 Mins
Cook Time: 14 Mins
Serves: 4

Ingredients:

- 300g Minced Pork
- 50g Onion (peeled and diced)
- 1Tsp Mustard
- 1Tsp Honey
- 1Tsp Garlic Puree
- 1Tbsp Cheddar Cheese (grated)
- Handful Fresh Basil (chopped into small pieces)
- Salt & Pepper

Directions:

1. In a bowl mix your meat, onion and seasoning until it is also mixed in well.
2. Form into balls.
3. Cook for 14 minutes on a 200°C temperature in your Air Fryer.
4. Serve!

Nutritional Value (Amount per Serving):

Calories: 182; Fat: 8.86; Carb: 4.41; Protein: 20.3

Chicken And Lamb Chop Karaage In An Air Fryer

Prep Time: 10 Mins
Cook Time: 20 Mins
Serves: 8

Ingredients:

- 4 Chicken drum sticks
- 4 Lamb chops
- Corn flour or potato starch
- Marinade sauce
- 2 Garlic cloves (Grated or finely chopped)
- 3 cm Ginger (Grated)
- 60 ml Soy sauce
- 1 table spoon Sesame oil
- 1 pinch Salt (Maldon salt)
- 1 table spoon Sake or white wine

Directions:

1. Mix all ingredients for marinade sauce in a bowl. Add the meat to the mixture and leave it for at least 10 minutes.
2. Coat the meat with corn flour. Place the meat in the baskets of the air fryer. Set to the "air fryer" mode, select 200°C and 20 mins. Press a start button.
3. After 10 mins, open the baskets and turn them over. Continue cooking for another 10 mins. See the results and extend the cooking time if needed. Ready to serve!!

Nutritional Value (Amount per Serving):

Calories: 651; Fat: 19.79; Carb: 2.94; Protein: 109.11

Chapter 4: Poultry

Fried Chicken Marinated In The Vietnamese Maggi Soy Sauce

Prep Time: 10 Mins
Cook Time: 25 Mins
Serves: 4

Ingredients:

- 8 Chicken drumsticks
- 5 table spoons Maggi seasoning sauce (Vietnamese style) or any soy sauce
- 2 table spoons Sesame oil
- 5 Garlic cloves (chopped)
- 1 piece Ginger

Directions:

1. Make some cut along side the bones so that the seasonings will soak faster and you can cook quicker. See the tip too!
2. Add soy sauce, sesame oil, ginger and garlic. Marinate the chicken.
3. Place the chicken in an air fryer. Choose "Air fryer" mode, set the temperature to 180 degrees and the time to 25 mins. After 10 mins, open the basket and turn over the chicken!
4. Enjoy!

Nutritional Value (Amount per Serving):

Calories: 495; Fat: 30.8; Carb: 2.62; Protein: 48.86

Air Fryer Frozen Whole Chicken

Prep Time: 2 Mins
Cook Time: 1 Hr 5 Mins
Serves: 4

Ingredients:

- 1.5 kg Frozen Medium Whole Chicken
- Extra Virgin Olive Oil Spray
- Salt & Pepper

Directions:

1. Place your frozen whole chicken in the air fryer basket, breast side up. Air fry for 20 minutes at 80°C or until almost thawed.
2. Then add extra virgin olive oil spray and spray all visible skin, then season with salt and pepper. Air fry for a further 25 minutes at 180°C.
3. Turn the chicken over using a fork.
4. Spray again and season again with salt and pepper.
5. Then air fry for a further 20 minutes at 180°C or until fully cooked.

Nutritional Value (Amount per Serving):

Calories: 258; Fat: 1.65; Carb: 55.57; Protein: 7.59

Air Fryer Chicken Wings

Prep Time: 5 Mins
Cook Time: 25 Mins
Serves: 4

Ingredients:

- 1 kg chicken wings
- ½ tsp garlic powder
- ½ tsp paprika
- ½ tsp salt
- ½ tsp black pepper
- 1 tbsp olive oil
- ½ tsp onion powder

Directions:

1. Preheat the air fryer at 180°C.
2. Prepare the chicken wings by firstly patting them dry with some kitchen roll. The dryer the chicken wings are, the crispier they will come out.
3. Add the wings to a large bowl and cover with the olive oil, tossing them so that they are all covered as much as possible.
4. Add all the seasonings, coating all the wings.
5. Put the chicken wings in the air fryer. Depending on how many wings you are cooking, and the size of your air fryer, you might need to do them in batches. You can also use a rack in your air fryer to fit more in. The key thing is to make sure the wings are not touching each other so that they have room to crisp up.
6. Cook for 20 minutes, turning and shaking 2 or 3 times to ensure they cook evenly.
7. Increase the temperature to 200°C and cook for a further 5 minutes or until the skin is crispy.
8. Serve with BBQ sauce, Hot Pepper Sauce, Buffalo Sauce

Nutritional Value (Amount per Serving):

Calories: 561; Fat: 35.11; Carb: 9.28; Protein: 49.35

Air Fryer BBQ Chicken Breast

Prep Time: 3 Mins
Cook Time: 20 Mins
Serves: 2

Ingredients:

- 2 chicken breasts 1 per person
- Salt and pepper
- Garlic salt or garlic powder
- 80 ml BBQ sauce
- Spray oil
- Smoked paprika

Directions:

1. Spray your chicken breasts with spray oil.
2. Sprinkle over smoked paprika, garlic salt and season well with salt and pepper too. Alternatively you can mix it all together beforehand and sprinkle on.
3. Turn over and repeat this step again.
4. Lay the chicken in the air fryer basket.
5. Cook at 180°C for 10 minutes.
6. Turn over the chicken breast.
7. Cook at 180°C for another 8 minutes.
8. Pour over the barbecue sauce; I like to use a silicone pastry brush to ensure even coverage, but you can just use a spoon or whatever you have to hand.
9. Cook at 180°C for another 2 minutes.
10. Check the internal temperature of the chicken breast (in the thickest part) is a minimum of 74°C and then remove.
11. You can rest for 5 minutes before you slice and serve. Or just serve up as a whole chicken breast alongside the rest of your dinner.

Nutritional Value (Amount per Serving):

Calories: 477; Fat: 15.95; Carb: 80.18; Protein: 20.21

Chicken Parmigiana Bake

Prep Time: 10 Mins
Cook Time: 30 Mins
Serves: 4

Ingredients:

- 4 small chicken breasts
- 4 slices Parma ham
- 1 tbsp olive oil
- 1 onion, finely chopped
- 1 garlic clove, grated
- 60g tomato puree
- 500g passata
- 100ml chicken stock,
- made with 1 stock cube
- ¼ tsp sugar
- 125g mozzarella ball,
- torn into pieces
- 40g grated Italian cheese
- Salt and black pepper

Directions:

1. Place each chicken breast between two pieces of cling film and bash with a rolling pin until each breast is about 2cm thick. Season with salt and black pepper
2. Wrap the Parma ham around the chicken lengthways and place the wrapped chicken on two air flow racks lined with parchment paper. Insert the air flow racks on the top and middle shelves of the air fryer and set the temperature to 180°C for 20 minutes, rotating the racks halfway through to ensure even cooking.
3. Meanwhile heat a frying pan with 1 tbsp oil, add the onion and fry gently for 5 minutes until softened but not coloured. Add the garlic and tomato

puree and cook for a minute. Pour in the passata and stock and season with salt and black pepper. Add the sugar and bring the sauce to the boil, then reduce the heat and simmer gently for 4-5 minutes until the sauce thickens.

4. Season the sauce then pour half into the base of a ceramic dish or roasting tin, place the chicken breasts on top and cover with the remaining sauce. Arrange the mozzarella on top, sprinkle over the parmesan then return to the air fryer for 10-15 minutes until the sauce is bubbling and the cheese has melted.

Nutritional Value (Amount per Serving):

Calories: 680; Fat: 34.12; Carb: 22.68; Protein: 69.01

Air-Fried Chicken

Prep Time: 2 Mins
Cook Time: 45 Mins
Serves: 4

Ingredients:

- 1 whole Chicken, chopped
- 1 T Fish sauce

Directions:

1. Pour fish sauce to the chicken.
2. Put to air-fryer for 45 minutes at 180°C.
3. Flip the chicken until all the sides are golden brown.

Nutritional Value (Amount per Serving):

Calories: 266; Fat: 6.44; Carb: 0.16; Protein: 48.71

Air Fryer Prawn Paste Chicken Wings

Prep Time: 10 Mins
Cook Time: 20 Mins
Serves: 3

Ingredients:

- 300g Mid-joint Chicken Wings or Drumlettes
- 2 tablespoon Olive Oil
- 1 tablespoon Prawn/Shrimp Paste
- 3/4 teaspoon Sugar
- 1 teaspoon Sesame Oil
- 1 teaspoon Ginger Juice
- 1/2 teaspoon Chinese Rice Wine / Sherry
- Corn Flour

Directions:

1. In a bowl, combine prawn paste, sugar, sesame oil, ginger juice and rice wine together until a paste is formed. Marinade chicken with the sauce for at least an hour or preferably overnight in the fridge.
2. Coat the marinated chicken with corn flour. Stir to coat evenly, shaking off excess flour on the chicken.
3. Preheat air fryer at 180°C. Meanwhile, lightly brush chicken pieces with olive oil.
4. Place the chickens into the air fryer. Cook for 8 minutes. Pull out the tray, use tongs to turn chicken pieces over, and cook for another 7 minutes. Drain cooked chicken on paper towels before serving.
5. Enjoy.

Nutritional Value (Amount per Serving):

Calories: 323; Fat: 23.38; Carb: 7.68; Protein: 20.14

Air Fryer Chicken Tikka

Prep Time: 5 Mins
Cook Time: 22 Mins
Serves: 2

Ingredients:

- 300 g chicken breast
- 2 peppers - (red and green)
- 1 medium white onion
- 3 tablespoon tikka seasoning
- 1 tablespoon olive oil

Directions:

1. Chop the peppers into chunks and thinly slice the onions.
2. Chop the chicken breasts in to chunks.
3. Add the peppers, onion, chicken, tikka seasoning and 1 tablespoon of olive oil to the air fryer.
4. Put on setting 6 for 22 minutes.

Nutritional Value (Amount per Serving):

Calories: 483; Fat: 24.89; Carb: 27.92; Protein: 34.2

Air-Fried Chicken Parmesan

Prep Time: 10 Mins
Cook Time: 20 Mins
Serves: 1

Ingredients:

- 1 thick chicken breast, cut in half
- 30g dried breadcrumbs
- 40g grated parmesan
- Salt to taste
- Cracked black pepper to taste
- 1/4 tsp mixed dried herbs
- 1 small egg, beaten
- Cooking spray
- 2 tbsp grated mozzarella
- 2-4 tsp Marinara sauce (I used the sauce attached)

Directions:

1. Mix together the breadcrumbs, parmesan cheese, mixed herbs, salt and pepper in a bowl. Set aside.
2. Using a meat tenderiser flatten the chicken pieces.
3. Preheat air fryer to 190°C for 3 minutes.
4. In the meantime dip the chicken in the egg then coat on all sides with the breadcrumb mixture. Spray both sides with cooking spray. Air-fry for 7 minutes, turning once. Note that times may varying.
5. Top each chicken piece with 1-2 teaspoons of marinara sauce then sprinkle with cheese. Air-fry for further 3 minutes or until cheese has melted.
6. Serve immediately with pasta or salad.

Nutritional Value (Amount per Serving):

Calories: 1131; Fat: 32.76; Carb: 52.44; Protein: 154.92

Air Fried Crispy Nugget Caprese

Prep Time: 10 Mins
Cook Time: 20 Mins
Serves: 6

Ingredients:

- 300g pack [Quorn Nuggets]
- 12 fresh basil leaves
- 12 mini mozzarella cheese balls
- 12 cherry tomatoes
- 2 tbsp balsamic glaze

Directions:

1. Set air-fryer to 200°C according to manufacturer's instructions. Place Quorn Crispy Nuggets in air fryer basket in batches if needed (do not overfill). Fry for 10 to 15 minutes or until golden brown, turning after 5 minutes.
2. Cut each crispy nugget in half. Thread half nugget, basil, mini mozzarella, cherry tomato and another half nugget onto a small skewer. Repeat to make 12 skewers. Place on serving tray.
3. Drizzle balsamic glaze over skewers before serving.

Nutritional Value (Amount per Serving):

Calories: 130; Fat: 6.44; Carb: 14.28; Protein: 6.15

Chapter 5: Casseroles, Frittatas, and Quiches

Spanish Omelette Using Air Fryer

Prep Time: 15 Mins
Cook Time: 30 Mins
Serves: 4

Ingredients:

- 4-5 medium size potatoes
- 5-6 eggs
- 1 onion
- Chorizo (optional and quantity up to you!)
- Extra virgin olive oil
- Salt

Directions:

1. Peel the potatoes, wash them and cut them into small cubes (also common in slices, but I do it in cubes, as my mum has always done). Cut also the onion into small cubes and also the chorizo (chorizo is optional, but it gives a very nice taste). Put everything in a bowl, add 2 tsp of virgin olive oil, some salt and mix it all
2. Pre-heat the air fryer (200°C 5 min). Once heated, add the potatoes, onion and the chorizo. Program the air fryer at 180°C for 25 min. Stir them from time to time (I normally do it each 5-6 min)
3. Beat the eggs while the potatoes are being cooked, salt them and put them in a bowl deep enough. Once the potatoes, onion and chorizo are ready, put them also in the bowl and mix everything
4. Take a non-stick frying pan (if possible special for omelettes) and put it at medium heat with a tiny bit of olive oil (1 tbsp, just enough to make sure the egg does not stick to it). Pour the mixture and wait a 3-4 of minutes until you feel the egg is curdling, moving the pan from time to time to make sure the egg does not stick
5. Once the egg is set, turn it over by placing a plate on the pan and turning the omelette over it with a smooth but firm turn. Slide back into the pan and let it curdle again on the other side. Feel free to choose the exact cooking time, it will all depend the way you want to see the egg once you serve the

tortilla. We like it quite raw at home...!!

Nutritional Value (Amount per Serving):

Calories: 590; Fat: 20.9; Carb: 76.77; Protein: 24.65

Courgette Fritters

Prep Time: 10 Mins
Cook Time: 15 Mins
Serves: 9

Ingredients:

- 100g Plain Flour
- 1 Medium Egg (beaten)
- 5Tbsp Milk
- 150g Grated Courgette
- 75g Onion (peeled and diced)
- 25g Cheddar Cheese (grated)
- 1Tbsp Mixed Herbs
- Salt & Pepper

Directions:

1. Put the plain flour into a bowl and add the seasoning.
2. Whisk the egg and milk and then add to the flour to make a smooth creamy batter.
3. Grate the courgette making sure to remove any excess moisture. Then add the onion.
4. Stir in the cheese.
5. If the batter isn't very thick then add more flour and cheese to it until it is of a reasonable thick mixture.
6. Make them into small burger shapes and place in the Air Fryer.
7. Cook on a 200°C heat for 20 minutes or until fully cooked.
8. Serve them with a good dollop of sour cream or mayonnaise.

Nutritional Value (Amount per Serving):

Calories: 131; Fat: 5.65; Carb: 12.66; Protein: 7.29

Air Fryer Corned Beef Pasty

Prep Time: 15 Mins
Cook Time: 12 Mins
Serves: 8

Ingredients:

- 400 g Leftover Corned Beef Hash
- 1 Large Egg
- 28 g Grated Cheddar Cheese
- 2 Tsp Tomato Puree
- 1 Tbsp Parsley
- Salt & Pepper
- 500 g Batch Air Fryer Pie Crust

Directions:

1. Place leftover corned beef hash in a bowl and mix with your hands to make it a little mushy. Cut up any bigger bits of potato. Add to the bowl the seasoning, the tomato puree and the grated cheese and mix well with your hands.
2. Crack egg into a bowl with salt and pepper and mix with a fork. Roll out your pastry and use the top of the pastry cutter to make perfect rounds.
3. Aim for making 6 pasty rounds and then place them on the worktop as you are going to be working in batches of two.
4. Place a pastry round in the pasty maker and fill one side with filling and then add egg wash around the edges.
5. Close the pasty maker and hold down tight to ensure it creates the perfect pasty.
6. Brush the pasty with egg wash.
7. Then place two pasties into the air fryer basket on the foil and air fry for 12 minutes at 180°C.

Nutritional Value (Amount per Serving):

Calories: 411; Fat: 25.02; Carb: 37.29; Protein: 9.48

Vegetarian Air Fryer Kimchi Bun

Prep Time: 10 Mins
Cook Time: 30 Mins
Serves: 4

Ingredients:

- 1 300g pack of Quorn Mince
- 1/2 cup chopped kimchi, save a splash of kimchi juice
- 2-3 chopped spring onions
- 1 egg
- 1 tbsp sesame oil
- 1 tbsp soy sauce
- 1 tsp white pepper powder
- Pinch of salt
- or The Dough:
- 480g flour
- 260ml warm water
- 2g salt

Directions:

1. Combine all the dough ingredients in a large bowl, mix well and shape into a ball. Let the dough rest for 10 minutes before kneading for 5 minutes and then resting for a further hour.
2. Mix all the remaining ingredients together, ensuring all liquid has been well absorbed by the Quorn Mince.
3. Lay out the dough on a lightly floured surface and cut into 16 equal pieces (about 30g/piece).
4. Wrap an equal amount of filling into each piece of dough, using your hands to form into a smooth and tightly wrapped bun.
5. Preheat air fryer to 180°C. Place the buns into the air fryer and spray some oil over the top of each bun, cook for 10-15 mins until golden and enjoy!

Nutritional Value (Amount per Serving):

Calories: 782; Fat: 12.86; Carb: 124.2; Protein: 43.64

Air Fryer Spinach Fritters

Prep Time: 15 Mins
Cook Time: 20 Mins
Serves: 4

Ingredients:

- 200g blanched spinach
- 2 boiled potatoes
- 1 tsp roasted cumin powder
- 1 tsp cumin seeds
- 1 tsp carom seeds
- 1 bunch chopped coriander leaves
- 1 tsp turmeric powder
- 1 tsp red chilli powder
- 1 tsp salt to taste
- 2 tbsp oil
- 4 tbsp gram flour for binding
- 1 tsp green chilli, ginger and garlic paste

Directions:

1. Take a bowl. Combine all the ingredients. Mix well and make a smooth dough.
2. From the dough mixture make small balls. Flatten with palm and brush oil in the pakoras. Keep aside
3. Preheat Air Fryer 180 the C for 5 minutes.
4. After 5 minutes. Take out the basket from Air Fryer. Brush oil in the basket. Place the pakora in the basket. Don't overcrowd it. It will break. Bake for 15 minutes. After 15 minutes take out from the basket. Apply oil in the pakora. Again bake for 5 minutes. Once it is done.
5. Transfer to a serving plate ready to serve hot spinach fritters with mustard sauce.

Nutritional Value (Amount per Serving):

Calories: 146; Fat: 7.71; Carb: 17.72; Protein: 3.24

Chapter 6: Desserts

Air Fryer Fat Rascals

Prep Time: 10 Mins
Cook Time: 11 Mins
Serves: 4

Ingredients:

- 120 g Self Raising Flour
- 120 g Plain Flour
- 100 g Unsalted Butter
- 40 g Caster Sugar
- 60 g Currants
- 60 g Mixed Peel
- 1 Medium Orange zest only
- 1 Medium Lemon zest only
- 1 Tbsp Vanilla Essence
- 1 Tsp Cinnamon
- 1 Tsp Mixed Spice
- Pinch Nutmeg
- 1 Small Egg beaten
- 2 Tbsp Skimmed Milk
- Glace Cherries for decoration

Directions:

1. Load into a bowl the flour, seasonings, and the sugar and then add in the butter chopped into chunks.
2. How To Make A Fat Rascal?
3. Mix the fat into the flour, seasonings, and sugar until you have a bowl of coarse brown coloured breadcrumbs.
4. How To Make A Fat Rascal?
5. Then add in the currants, peel, and the zest, along with the vanilla essence and mix well.
6. Next add enough milk to make a soft scone style dough.
7. Then measure out your mix and then divide by four. Then weigh out your dough to make 4 equal sized dough balls. Then make into scone shapes.
8. Decorate the tops with glace cherry halves for eyes, mixed peel for nose and then raisins for a smile.
9. Brush the tops of the rascals with egg wash using a pastry brush.
10. Load into the air fryer and air fry for 8 minutes at 180°C followed by 3 minutes at 160°C.

Nutritional Value (Amount per Serving):

Calories: 408; Fat: 15.84; Carb: 55.92; Protein: 9.23

Air Fryer Giant Doughnut Cake

Prep Time: 2 Mins
Cook Time: 20 Mins
Serves: 8

Ingredients:

- 500 g Bread Maker Doughnut Dough
- 240 ml Icing Sugar
- 45 ml Whole Milk
- 1 Tsp Vanilla Essence
- Food Colouring for glaze

Directions:

1. Load your bread machine doughnut dough into the bread maker and get it started.
2. When the bread machine beeps dump the doughnut dough into your mould. Load the mould into the air fryer basket.
3. Cook for 10 minutes at 180°C. Followed by a further 10 minutes at 160°C.
4. Remove the mould from the air fryer and remove the giant doughnut cake from the mould and allow to cool for 5 minutes.
5. Mix milk and icing sugar together in a bowl until you have a doughnut glaze. Add food colouring and stir. Brush your glaze over your giant doughnut and add sprinkles. Allow to set and then serve.

Nutritional Value (Amount per Serving):

Calories: 295; Fat: 6.23; Carb: 39.82; Protein: 19.17

Quick Simple Air Fryer Fruit Crumble

Prep Time: 15 Mins
Cook Time: 15 Mins
Serves: 6

Ingredients:

- 75g Plain Flour
- 33g Butter
- 30g Caster Sugar
- 1 Medium Red Apple
- 4 Medium Plums
- 50g Frozen Berries
- 1Tsp Cinnamon

Directions:

1. Preheat your air fryer to 180°C.
2. In a suitable dish that will fit in your air fryer add your fruit. Peel and dice everything and make sure it is all of a similar size so that it will cook evenly.
3. Now make your crumble – Place plain flour in a mixing bowl along with sugar and mix in the butter. Rub the fat into the flour until the mixture resembles breadcrumbs.
4. Place the crumble mixture over the fruit and place in the air fryer.
5. Cook in the air fryer for 15 minutes at 180°C.
6. Serve!

Nutritional Value (Amount per Serving):

Calories: 133; Fat: 3.56; Carb: 24.19; Protein: 2.03

Air Fryer 10 Minutes Smartie Cookies

Prep Time: 5 Mins
Cook Time: 5 Mins
Serves: 9

Ingredients:

- 100g Butter
- 225g Self Raising Flour
- 5Tbsp Milk
- 3Tbsp Cocoa
- 1/3 Tube Of Smarties
- 50g White Chocolate
- 100g Caster Sugar
- 1Tsp Vanilla Essence

Directions:

1. Preheat the air fryer to 180°C.
2. Mix the cocoa, flour and sugar in a large mixing bowl.
3. Rub in the butter and add the vanilla essence and mix really well.
4. Using a rolling pin smash up your white chocolate so that they are a mix of medium and really small chocolate chips.
5. Add the chocolate and the milk to your cookie mix and mix well.
6. Knead your mixture well until it is nice and soft and add a little more milk if you need to.
7. Roll out your mixture and using a cookie cutter form into nice biscuit shapes.
8. Place the Smarties into the top of the cookies so that they are half in the cookie and half out in the open.
9. Place the cookies into the air fryer on a baking sheet and cook for ten minutes at 180°C.
10. Serve with warm milk.

Nutritional Value (Amount per Serving):

Calories: 185; Fat: 7.27; Carb: 25.55; Protein: 3.81

Air Fryer Brownies

Prep Time: 5 Mins
Cook Time: 30 Mins
Serves: 2

Ingredients:

- 100 g caster sugar
- 40 g cocoa powder
- 30 g plain flour
- 1/4 tsp. baking powder
- Pinch salt
- 60 g butter, melted and cooled slightly
- 1 large egg

Directions:

1. Grease a 15cm round cake pan with cooking spray. In a medium bowl, whisk to combine sugar, cocoa powder, flour, baking powder, and salt.
2. In a small bowl, whisk melted butter and egg until combined. Add wet ingredients to dry ingredients and stir until combined.
3. Transfer brownie batter to prepared cake pan and smooth top. Cook in air fryer at 180°C for 16-18 minutes. Let cool 10 minutes before slicing.

Nutritional Value (Amount per Serving):

Calories: 931; Fat: 57; Carb: 92.15; Protein: 14.37

Bread Machine Doughnuts Dough

Prep Time: 3 Mins
Cook Time: 23 Mins
Serves: 6

Ingredients:

- 450 g Plain Flour
- 140 ml Whole Milk
- 1 Large Egg
- 50 g Caster Sugar
- 50 g Butter
- 1.5 Tsp Dried Yeast
- 1 Tsp Cinnamon
- 1 Tsp Nutmeg
- 1 Tsp Vanilla Essence
- 1 Tsp Salt

Directions:

1. Add your milk and 6tbsp of water into your bread machine. Crack in an egg.
2. Add in your dry ingredients making sure that the yeast goes in last and that it is placed on top. Also make sure that the plain flour covers the wet ingredients. Also make sure that the dry ingredients are spread out and not all dumped in one corner of the bread machine. Add in seasonings including the vanilla essence.
3. Place the lid down on your bread machine and set the time to 23 minutes on the dough setting.
4. When it beeps roll out your doughnut dough on a clean worktop. Flour the dough and the rolling pin so that it doesn't stick.
5. Using doughnut cutters make into doughnut shapes.

Nutritional Value (Amount per Serving):

Calories: 361; Fat: 6.96; Carb: 63.17; Protein: 9.72

Lime Drizzle Loaf

Prep Time: 10 Mins
Cook Time: 40 Mins
Serves: 8

Ingredients:

- 130g Butter
- 130g Caster Sugar
- 130g Self Raising Flour
- 2 Eggs
- 2 Limes, Zest only
- 2 Juice of Limes
- 60g Caster Sugar

Directions:

1. Add the Butter and Sugar to a bowl and beat till creamy. Around 5 minutes.
2. Add the Eggs one at a time, beating after each addition until fully incorporated.
3. Sieve in the Self Raising Flour and fold in along with the Lime Zest.
4. Line a loaf tin with greaseproof paper or a loaf liner or use a rectangular metal takeaway container.
5. Add the Cake batter and level out.
6. Preheat the Ninja Foodi max Health Grill & Air Fryer.
7. Set to 150°C and bake for 40 minutes.
8. Once it is ready, place the loaf tin in the centre and leave to bake.
9. Check that the cake is baked through by inserting a skewer into the middle and ensuring that is comes out clean.
10. Meanwhile mix the Lime Juice and Sugar together in a bowl.
11. Use a cocktail stick/skewer or fork to prick holes all over the cake and pour over the drizzle.
12. Leave the cake in the tin until it is cool before removing.

Nutritional Value (Amount per Serving):

Calories: 200; Fat: 11.61; Carb: 19.78; Protein: 4.97

Air Fryer Doughnuts From Scratch

Prep Time: 5 Mins
Cook Time: 8 Mins
Serves: 7

Ingredients:

- 500 g Bread Maker Doughnut Dough
- 240 ml Icing Sugar
- 40 ml Whole Milk
- 1 Tsp Vanilla Essence
- Extra Virgin Olive Oil Spray
- Plain Flour for rolling
- Food Colouring for glaze
- 100 's and 1000's for sprinkling

Directions:

1. Remove your doughnut dough from the bread maker and roll out on a floured worktop. Add a little extra flour to the rolling pin to prevent it sticking.
2. Using your biscuit cutters cut out the big doughnut shapes. Then cut out using a smaller cutter the doughnut holes. Put the doughnut holes to one side.
3. Load up to 4 doughnuts into the air fryer basket and cook for 8 minutes at 180°C. Though after 4 minutes spray with extra virgin olive oil to help with the golden glow.
4. Mix milk and icing sugar together in a bowl until you have a thick glaze. Add food colouring or separate into ramekins if doing different coloured doughnuts. Sprinkle with 100's and 1000's and eat.

Nutritional Value (Amount per Serving):

Calories: 388; Fat: 9.84; Carb: 48.46; Protein: 25.61

The Ultimate Air Fryer Pumpkin

Prep Time: 5 Mins
Cook Time: 10 Mins
Serves: 9

Ingredients:

- 3Tbsp Pumpkin Filling
- 1 Sheet Puff Pastry
- 1 Small Egg (beaten)

Directions:

1. Preheat your air fryer to 180°C.
2. Roll out a sheet of puff pastry and layer it with pumpkin pie filling making sure there is a 1cm gap around the edges.
3. Cut it up into 9 square pieces.
4. Cover the gaps with beaten egg so that you will have that lovely egg glow.
5. Place in the air fryer on a baking sheet for 12 minutes at 180°C.
6. Serve!

Nutritional Value (Amount per Serving):

Calories: 49; Fat: 3.6; Carb: 2.75; Protein: 1.64

Air Fryer Doughnuts

Prep Time: 30 Mins
Cook Time: 25 Mins
Serves: 6-8

Ingredients:

- 125ml milk, lukewarm
- 50g unsalted butter, melted and cooled to lukewarm
- 7g sachet dried fast-action yeast
- 60g caster sugar
- 1 tsp vanilla extract
- 275g plain flour, plus extra for dusting
- ½ tsp ground cinnamon (optional)
- 1 egg, beaten
- For the glaze
- 125g icing sugar
- 3 tbsp milk
- ¼ tsp vanilla extract
- flavourless oil, for proving

Directions:

1. Combine the milk, melted butter, yeast, 1 tsp of the sugar and the vanilla extract in the bowl of a stand mixer. Leave for 8-10 mins for the yeast to activate.
2. In a separate bowl, combine the remaining sugar, flour, ½ tsp salt and the cinnamon, if using. Mix the beaten egg into the milk mixture, then fold in the dry ingredients. Knead with a dough hook on a medium speed for 5-8 mins until the dough is smooth and elastic. You can also knead by hand for 10-12 mins, until smooth. It's a very sticky dough, so be patient with it.
3. Transfer to a lightly oiled bowl, cover with a clean tea towel and leave in a warm place for 1 hr 30 mins until the dough has doubled in size. Tip the dough out onto a lightly floured surface and roll out to around 1.5cm thick.

Cut out your doughnuts using a doughnut cutter or two cutters (1 x 7.5cm and 1 x 2.5cm for the middle). Put the doughnuts on a lined baking sheet, along with the doughnut centres, if you like, and cover with a clean tea towel. Leave to rise for 40 mins or overnight in the fridge (the doughnuts will hold their shape better if proved in the fridge).

4. When ready to cook, place 2-3 doughnuts (and their centres, if keeping) in the air-fryer basket and cook at 180°C for 5-6 mins, following manufacturer's instructions, until golden. (Bear in mind that some air fryers generate more intense heat, so keep checking to make sure the doughnuts don't burn.) Remove from the basket and leave to cool on a wire rack while you cook the remaining doughnuts. You can place a sheet of baking parchment at the bottom of your basket if you're worried about the doughnuts sticking and to prevent indents from the basket forming on the doughnuts.
5. While the final batch is cooking, sift the icing sugar into a bowl and stir in the milk and vanilla extract. When the doughnuts have cooled, dip the top of each one in the glaze. Leave on the wire rack for the glaze to set. Best eaten on the day but will keep for up to 24 hours in an airtight container.

Nutritional Value (Amount per Serving):

Calories: 653; Fat: 26.54; Carb: 81.45; Protein: 22

Air Fryer Pop Tarts

Prep Time: 1 Min
Cook Time: 3 Mins
Serves: 2

Ingredients:

- 2 pop tarts

Directions:
1. Turn the air fryer on to 200°C. No need to pre-heat.
2. Layer the pop tarts in a single layer, 1-2 in the air fryer basket.
3. Cook for 3 minutes.
4. Serve and enjoy immediately. Be careful – they're VERY hot!

Nutritional Value (Amount per Serving):

Calories: 193; Fat: 3.11; Carb: 39.94; Protein: 2.07

Pumpkin Loaf Cake

Prep Time: 20 Mins
Cook Time: 15 Mins
Serves: 10

Ingredients:

- 125g Plain Flour
- 1 tsp Baking Powder
- 1/2 tsp Bicarbonate of Soda
- 1 tsp ground Cinnamon
- 1 tsp ground Cloves
- 1/4 tsp ground Nutmeg
- 1/2 tsp Salt
- 200g Light Brown Sugar
- 80g Olive Oil
- 1 Egg
- 400g Pumpkin Puree

Directions:

1. Mix all of the ingredients together with a whisk in a large bowl.
2. Line a loaf tin with a loaf liner or greaseproof paper.
3. Add batter to tin.
4. Air fry at 170°C for 20 minutes.
5. Open the lid, brush over butter and add sugar.
6. Air fry for a further 10 – 15 minutes.

Nutritional Value (Amount per Serving):

Calories: 377; Fat: 22.02; Carb: 35.72; Protein: 14.28

Air Fry Banana In Syrup And Nutella

Prep Time: 2 Mins
Cook Time: 10 Mins
Serves: 1

Ingredients:

- 2-3 banana, sliced (use up ripped)
- Toppings
- Maple Syrup
- Nutella
- Butter (optional)

Directions:

1. Place banana in the air fryer. Set it for 180°C for 10 min. Open to turn over half way.
2. Once cooked in air fryer, plate up and too with maple syrup, honey or Nutella or on its own with a little bit of butter.

Nutritional Value (Amount per Serving):

Calories: 1520; Fat: 33.11; Carb: 317.04; Protein: 14.47

Apple Pie Bombs Baked In An Air

Prep Time: 50 Mins
Cook Time: 10 Mins
Serves: 10

Ingredients:

- or The Apple Pie Filling
- 30 g unsalted butter
- 50 g brown sugar
- 80ml water
- or The Outer Crust
- 110 g granulated sugar
- 1 tsp cinnamon
- 50 g unsalted butter, melted
- 10 homemade buttermilk biscuits
- 2 apples, cored and chopped
- 2 tbsp corn starch
- 1 tsp cinnamon

Directions:

1. In a pot, add in all the ingredients for the apple pie filling. Cook on medium heat for 2-3 mins, stirring constantly.
2. Simmer the sauce for another 30 seconds or until desired consistency. Let it cool down before making the bombs.
3. On a floured work surface, use floured fingers or a rolling pin to flatten the homemade buttermilk biscuits.
4. Place the cooled apple pie filling in the centre, then wrap it into a ball shape. Repeat the steps for the remaining bombs
5. Dip the bombs into melted butter and cinnamon sugar and transfer them into an air fryer.
6. Air-fry the bombs at 190°C for 10 mins.
7. After baked, let the bombs cool down for 5-10 mins before serving.

Nutritional Value (Amount per Serving):

Calories: 295; Fat: 10.3; Carb: 47.97; Protein: 4.04

Healthier Peanut Butter Cookies With Air Fryer

Prep Time: 10 Mins
Cook Time: 20 Mins
Serves: 15

Ingredients:

- 70 g unsweetened peanut butter
- 30 g almond flour
- ~1 g vanilla extract
- 15 g maple syrup/ honey

Directions:

1. Mix wet ingredients all together in a bowl.
2. Add almond flour into wet mixtures.
3. Leave to cool in the fridge for 5-10 mins (i find this helps me to roll the dough into balls).
4. Make 15 small dough balls and flatten them with fork.
5. Bake in air fryer 170°C for 15 mins. Then flip side for another 5 mins.

Nutritional Value (Amount per Serving):

Calories: 26; Fat: 1.75; Carb: 2.14; Protein: 0.72

Chapter 7: Wraps and Sandwiches

My Battered Fish Finger Sandwich

Prep Time: 2 Mins
Cook Time: 8 Mins
Serves: 1

Ingredients:

- 6 Battered FISH Fingers
- 2 Slices Bread Buttered
- Salt and Vinegar

Directions:

1. Cook in air fryer for 8 minutes turning them over or grill them.
2. Butter the Bread and lay the fish fingers across the bread.
3. Add salt and Vinegar then add the top slice of bread.
4. Cut in half serve and Enjoy.

Nutritional Value (Amount per Serving):

Calories: 1212; Fat: 64.97; Carb: 19.91; Protein: 127.73

Air Fryer Mcchicken Sandwich

Prep Time: 5 Mins
Cook Time: 14 Mins
Serves: 4

Ingredients:

- 4 Chicken Breasts
- 2 Tsp Oregano
- reading Production Lime
- Beaten Egg Bowl
- cchicken Garnish
- Shredded Lettuce
- 2 Tbsp Mayonnaise
- 1 Tsp Dill Pickle Juice
- 1 Tsp Mustard
- 2 Tsp Basil
- Salt & Pepper
- Flour Bowl
- Breadcrumbs Bowl
- 4 Burger Buns

Directions:

1. Set up your production line with a flour bowl, beaten egg bowl and breadcrumbs bowl.
2. Pound your chicken breasts by adding them to a Ziploc bag and banging them with a rolling pin to flatten them out.
3. Then use a large cookie cutter to cut the chicken breast into rounds.
4. Then season your chicken with salt, pepper, oregano, and basil.
5. Then load the chicken into the flour, then the egg and then the breadcrumbs until well coated.
6. Place the chicken into the air fryer basket and air fry for 14 minutes at 180°C.
7. Mix mayonnaise with dill pickle juice and mustard and then load the chicken burgers into buns with shredded lettuce and the flavoured mayo before serving.

Nutritional Value (Amount per Serving):

Calories: 1032; Fat: 46.76; Carb: 64.07; Protein: 85.22

Quorn Korean Crunchy Fillet Sandwich

Prep Time: 10 Mins
Cook Time: 15 Mins
Serves: 2

Ingredients:

- 1 package Quorn Crunchy Fillet Burger
- 2 vegan brioche buns, lightly toasted
- picy Mayo:
- ½ cup (around 8 tbsp) vegan mayo
- 2 tablespoons gochujang
- or Serving:
- Gherkins
- Kimchi
- Spring onions
- 40g shredded cabbage

Directions:

1. Pre-heat air fryer to 200°C. Place frozen Quorn Crunchy Fillet Burger in air fryer and cook for 6 minutes. Flip the burger and continue to cook for another 6 minutes.
2. Meanwhile, lightly toast the vegan brioche buns.
3. While the buns are toasting, whisk together vegan mayo and gochujang to make spicy mayo,
4. Assemble the sandwich: spread spicy mayo on bottom bun, add spring onions and gherkins, then place crunch fillet burger on top. Add kimchi and extra spring onions. Add top bun slathered with spicy mayo.

Nutritional Value (Amount per Serving):

Calories: 608; Fat: 24.4; Carb: 88.39; Protein: 9.65

Sandwich

Prep Time: 10 Mins
Cook Time: 30 Mins
Serves: 2

Ingredients:

- 2 Quorn Southern Fried Burgers
- 1/4 cup mayonnaise
- 4 tsp apple cider vinegar
- 1 tsp grainy mustard
- 1 tsp honey
- 1 clove garlic, minced
- 1/4 tsp each salt and pepper
- 1 cup packed shredded kale leaves
- 1/4 cup sriracha sauce
- 2 soft bread buns, toasted
- 8 gherkins, sliced

Directions:

1. Set air fryer to 200°C according to manufacturer's instructions. Generously grease air fryer basket. Place Quorn Southern Fried Burgers in air fryer basket. Fry, turning after 5 minutes, for 10 to 12 minutes or until golden brown.
2. Meanwhile, make the kale slaw by stirring together the mayonnaise, vinegar, mustard, honey, garlic, salt and pepper; toss with kale until well coated.
3. Just before serving, toss burgers with sriracha. Assemble in bread buns with kale slaw and gherkins.

Nutritional Value (Amount per Serving):

Calories: 296; Fat: 14.87; Carb: 24.97; Protein: 15.89

Air Fryer Yorkshire Pudding Wrap

Prep Time: 2 Mins
Cook Time: 4 Mins
Serves: 2

Ingredients:

- 400 g Leftover Roast Dinner
- 2 Giant Yorkshire Puddings frozen

Directions:

1. Place your frozen Yorkshire pudding in the air fryer and cook for 1 minute at 180°C.
2. Flatten the Yorkshire pudding with either your hand or a rolling pin.
3. Load the Yorkshire pudding with a mix of your leftovers and then place the loaded Yorkshire pudding back in the air fryer.
4. Air fry for a further 3 minutes at 180°C or until piping hot. Fold your Yorkshire pudding in half to transform into a wrap before tucking in.

Nutritional Value (Amount per Serving):

Calories: 426; Fat: 27; Carb: 13.8; Protein: 32

Chapter : Appetizers and Snacks

Air-Fryer Aubergine, Feta And Mushroom Roast

Prep Time: 5 Mins
Cook Time: 25 Mins
Serves: 2

Ingredients:

- 1 aubergine
- 1 portabella mushroom
- Chilli flakes
- 1 small block of Feta cheese
- 1 onion
- seasoning - salt
- tamarind sauce

Directions:

1. Slice your Aubergine into thick discs, Spray or lightly coat in olive oil. season well with salt. Add them to your air fryer and roast at 180°C for 15 minutes.
2. We have an air fry with two compartments so two different things can be cooked at once separately. If you have an air fryer that is only one large component then you could wait till the aubergine has finished cooking and then remove and add your other ingredients to do the second part. Ir if cooking this in a conventional oven then just pla
3. Slice your mushroom and onion and add to the air fryer. Sprinkle with a few chilli flakes. Chop your feta cheese into chunky cubes and place on top of the onion and mushroom. Drizzle over a little tamarind sauce. If you don't have tamarind sauce try any other sticky sauce or sticky vinegar. I think sriracha sauce would work great for this. Place in the fryer and roast at 150 for 10 minutes.
4. Remove the aubergine from the fryer and put it on a plate. the air fryer makes them crispy and crunchy around the edges and juicy and roasted in the middle. Very gently remove the veg and cheese when they are done and pile them on top of the discs. The cheese will be creamy and soft in the middle but still retain its cube shape. As it cools they will crumble. The onion was sweet and caramelised but still with a little crunch.
5. Drizzle over some more tamarind sauce and enjoy! perfect.

Nutritional Value (Amount per Serving):

Calories: 955; Fat: 20.93; Carb: 154.97; Protein: 37.83

Air Fryer Frozen Tempura Shrimp

Prep Time: 1 Mins
Cook Time: 8 Mins
Serves: 2

Ingredients:

- 12 Frozen Tempura Shrimp
- Olive Oil Spray

Directions:

1. Place your frozen tempura shrimp into the air fryer basket.
2. Spray with extra virgin olive oil for extra crisp.
3. Air fry tempura for 8 minutes at 180°C.
4. Your tempura shrimp will now be perfectly crispy and ready for serving.

Nutritional Value (Amount per Serving):

Calories: 1758; Fat: 44.17; Carb: 207.89; Protein: 131.55

Loaded Potato Skins With Garlic And Sour Cream Dip

Prep Time: 10 Mins
Cook Time: 70 Mins
Serves: 4

Ingredients:

- 4 medium baking potatoes
- (about 700g)

- 1 tbsp vegetable oil
- Salt
- 1 tbsp butter
- 125g mature cheddar, grated
- 3 spring onions
- 200g can sweetcorn, drained
- 1 tsp Dijon mustard
- Dip
- 150ml sour cream
- 1 small bunch chives,
- finely chopped

Directions:

1. Wash and dry the potatoes then prick the skin a few times with a fork. Rub the potatoes with oil, then rub in a little salt. Place the potatoes on an air flow rack and set the air fryer temperature to 200°C. Bake for 1 hour, turning the potatoes halfway through to ensure that they are evenly cooked. The potatoes should be completely tender when pierced with a skewer or sharp knife.
2. Remove the potatoes from the air fryer and carefully cut the potatoes in half and allow to cool slightly before scooping out most of the flesh into a large mixing bowl, being careful to keep the skins intact.
3. Mash the potatoes with the butter then stir though 100g cheese, ¾ of the spring onions, sweetcorn and Dijon mustard. Season then fill the potatoes evenly with the mashed potato mixture.
4. Transfer the potato skins onto two air flow racks and sprinkle over the remaining cheese. Pop potato skins on the top and middle shelves and cook for a further 10 minutes until the cheese is bubbling. Rotate the trays halfway through for even browning.
5. To serve, pop the sour cream and chives into a small bowl and mix to combine. Arrange the potato skins on a serving plate, sprinkle over the remaining spring onions and serve with the sour cream dip on the side.

Nutritional Value (Amount per Serving):

Calories: 555; Fat: 21.74; Carb: 10.28; Protein: 76.29

Ninja Foodi Roast Potatoes

Prep Time: 10 Mins
Cook Time: 27 Mins
Serves: 4

Ingredients:

- 1kg Maris Pipers or King Edwards
- 500ml boiling water
- 1tbsp olive oil – or oil/fat of your choice
- Salt and pepper
- Optional seasoning – rosemary, sage, thyme and or garlic

Directions:

1. Peel and quarter the potatoes. Rinse them under some water before placing in the air fryer basket of the Ninja Foodi.
2. Pour 500ml of boiling water in the cooking pot of the Ninja Foodi before placing the basket inside.
3. Place the pressure cooker lid on the Ninja Foodi and select high pressure for 2 minutes. Remember to check the valve is in the seal position.
4. When the pressure cooker has finished, perform a quick release before carefully removing the lid.
5. Take the basket with the potatoes in them out of the Ninja Foodi, taking care not to burn your hands.
6. Give the potatoes a gentle shake to fluff them up - this will help to crisp them up.
7. Pour the water from the Ninja Foodi pot.
8. Drizzle the oil over the potatoes, you might need to use a brush to make sure they are all covered. You may prefer to transfer the potatoes to a larger bowl if you find there is not enough space to oil them up in the basket.
9. Season with your choice of herbs, or just with salt and pepper if preferred.
10. Return the seasoned potatoes to the Ninja Foodi cooking pot (in the basket) and close the lid.

11. Select the air fryer function and cook at 200°C for 25 minutes, checking on them 3 or 4 times and turning to make sure they are evenly crisped up.

Nutritional Value (Amount per Serving):

Calories: 2689; Fat: 53.64; Carb: 414.72; Protein: 136.69

Methi Pakoda With Air Fryer

Prep Time: 10 Mins
Cook Time: 10 Mins
Serves: 4

Ingredients:

- 150g chopped methi
- 1 onion chopped
- 2 tbsp gram flour
- 1/2 tsp turmeric powder
- 1 tsp red chilli powder
- 1/2 tsp roasted cumin powder
- to taste Salt
- 1 tsp oil

Directions:

1. Wash methi properly and chopped finely. Keep aside.
2. In a bowl combined all the ingredients, oil and salt. Mix well. Add needed water to make a dough. Keep aside.
3. Pre heat Air Fryer for 180 degree C. Make a small size ball and flatten it. Apply oil in the basket and place the pakoda and bake for 10 minutes.
4. Once it is done. Transfer to a serving plate. Serve immediately hot methi pakoda with Tomato ketchup.

Nutritional Value (Amount per Serving):

Calories: 105; Fat: 5.38; Carb: 3.63; Protein: 10.05

Aberdeen Angus Burgers

Prep Time: 10 Mins
Cook Time: 30 Mins
Serves: 4

Ingredients:

- 500g Aberdeen Angus
- minced beef
- 20g Panko breadcrumbs
- 1 tbsp water
- Vegetable oil spray
- 60g cheese, grated
- 400g frozen skinny fries
- 4 brioche burger buns,
- sliced
- 4 tbsps mayonnaise
- 1 Baby Gem lettuce
- 1 beef tomato, 4 thick slices
- Side salad of your choice
- Salt and pepper to taste

Directions:

1. For the burgers, put the minced beef, breadcrumbs and water into a mixing bowl and add a pinch of salt and pepper. Mix with your hands until combined, then roll into 4 equal sized balls. Flatten the burgers to about 1cm thickness, then spray lightly with oil on both sides.
2. Insert the 10-in-1 wire rack into the air fryer with the grill plate, ridge side up, on top of the rack. Set the temperature to 200°C and preheat the grill plate for 3 minutes.
3. Next place the burgers onto the hot grill plate and cook for 14 minutes, or until cooked to your liking, turning halfway through.
4. When the burgers are ready, transfer them to a warm plate, top them with

the grated cheese then cover with foil to keep warm. Take the rack and grill plate out of the air fryer and put onto a heat proof surface to cool. Wear oven gloves to remove the wire rack and grill plate from the air fryer, as they will be very hot.

5. Arrange the fries on two air flow racks and place on the top and middle shelves of the air fryer. Set the air fryer temperature to 190°C and cook for 12 minutes, rotating the racks halfway through for even browning.
6. When the chips have 3 minutes left to cook, pop the burger buns on to an airflow rack to warm.
7. To assemble, spread a spoonful of mayonnaise over the base of each burger bun, top with lettuce and tomato. Carefully place the burger on top, then add the lid. Serve with the skinny fries and a side salad.

Nutritional Value (Amount per Serving):

Calories: 1449; Fat: 69.36; Carb: 91.96; Protein: 115.26

My Baked Jacket Potato With Coronation Chicken

Prep Time: 3 Mins
Cook Time: 16 Mins
Serves: 1

Ingredients:

- 1 large size potato washed and pricked with a fork
- 3 tbls Coronation Chicken
- 1 tsp Butter
- 1 little salt

Directions:

1. Wash and prick the potato all around. Add to the air fryer for 15 minutes/200°C.
2. When the potato is soft right through cut a cross through the potato but not right to the bottom and then pull apart a little. Add the butter to melt through and a little salt. Then add the Coronation chicken inside and on top.
3. Or you can scrape out the soft potato inside and mix with the Coronation chicken then add back inside the potato. Then warm up again for 1 minute in air fryer.
4. Either way is good. Serve and Enjoy.

Nutritional Value (Amount per Serving):

Calories: 865; Fat: 19.67; Carb: 33.62; Protein: 130.68

Air Fryer Potatoes And Sausage

Prep Time: 15 Mins
Cook Time: 20 Mins
Serves: 4

Ingredients:

- 1 kg potatoes
- 1 medium brown onion
- 1 Tablespoon all-purpose seasoning
- ½ Tablespoon garlic granules
- Salt and pepper to taste
- 400 g Kielbasa sausages
- 2 Tablespoon olive oil

Directions:

1. Preheat your air fryer to 180°C.
2. Peel and dice the potatoes into small bite-sized cubes and add them to a large bowl of cold water. Rinse the potatoes a few times under cold running water until the water is clear.
3. Pat the potatoes dry with a kitchen towel and transfer to a large bowl. Season the potatoes with all purpose seasoning, garlic granules, salt, black pepper and half of the olive oil. Mix or toss to combine.
4. Add the seasoned potatoes to the preheated air fryer basket and air fry for 10 - 12 minutes shaking the basket halfway. The potatoes should be fork-tender and about 90-95% done at this point.
5. While the potatoes are cooking, slice the kielbasa on bias or rounds and about 1-2cm thick, and chop the onions into big chunks. Separate the onions if you could then transfer them to a bowl along with the kielbasa, add the remaining olive oil and mix to combine.
6. Add the sausages and onions to the potatoes and carefully mix to combine. Continue to air fry for another 5-8 minutes flipping halfway. Serve and enjoy!

Nutritional Value (Amount per Serving):

Calories: 416; Fat: 16; Carb: 49; Protein: 20

Air Fryer Fish Chips

Prep Time: 10 Mins
Cook Time: 15 Mins
Serves: 4

Ingredients:

- My Air Fryer Chips
- 2 Fish Fillets (catfish is best)
- 1 Medium Egg (beaten)
- 3 Slices Wholemeal Bread (made into breadcrumbs)
- 25g Bag Tortilla Chips
- 1 Lemon (rind and juice)
- 1Tbsp Parsley
- Salt & Pepper

Directions:

1. Make the chips just like my Air Fryer chips recipe (see page 5).
2. Cut the fish fillets in half to make four nice sized pieces of fish ready for cooking. Season with lemon juice and then put to one side.
3. Grind in a food processor the breadcrumbs, lemon rind, parsley, tortillas and salt and pepper. Place it into a large baking tray.
4. Cover the fish in the beaten egg and then in the breadcrumbs mixture.
5. Then cook for 15 minutes on 180°C until nice and crispy and when the lovely fish smell fills your kitchen.

Nutritional Value (Amount per Serving):

Calories: 209; Fat: 9.1; Carb: 16.69; Protein: 14.7

Air Fryer Frozen Chicken Nuggets

Prep Time: 3 Mins
Cook Time: 10 Mins
Serves: 5

Ingredients:

- 30 frozen chicken nuggets

Directions:

1. Preheat the air fryer to 200°C for 3-5 minutes.
2. Place frozen chicken nuggets in the air fryer basket, spreading them out in a single layer. No need to spray with oil.
3. Air fry the frozen chicken nuggets for 8-10 minutes at 200°C shaking the basket or flipping the nuggets halfway through (optional) until golden brown and cooked through.
4. Remove from the air fryer and serve with your favorite dipping sauce.

Nutritional Value (Amount per Serving):

Calories: 1051; Fat: 72.14; Carb: 49; Protein: 51.59

Chapter 9: Sauces, Dips, and Dressings

Creamy Vegan Tahini Salad Dressing

Prep Time: 2 Mins
Cook Time: 2 Mins
Serves: 4

Ingredients:

- 2 tablespoons tahini
- 3 tablespoons vegan mayo
- 2 tablespoons lemon juice
- 2 teaspoons maple syrup (or agave nectar, but remember it's sweeter)
- 1 teaspoon dried parsley
- 2 tablespoons water
- 1 pinch salt and pepper (not too much salt)

Directions:

1. Add all the ingredients to a clean jam jar or another jar with a tight lid and shake well until cmbined. You might need to use a teaspoon to help along any bits in the bottom of the jar.
2. Add 2 tablespoons of water, Sounds odd, but trust me. Now put the lid back on and shake like crazy.
3. Taste for seasoning and to check the consistency, you can add a little more water if you want it a bit thinner.
4. Keep it in the fridge until you need it and give it a good shake before serving.
5. Enjoy!

Nutritional Value (Amount per Serving):

Calories: 99; Fat: 7.81; Carb: 6.84; Protein: 1.55

Best Turkey Marinade

Prep Time: 5 Mins
Cook Time: 2 Mins
Serves: 1

Ingredients:

- ½ tablespoon Paprika
- 1 teaspoon Oregano
- 1.5 teaspoon Thyme
- ½ tablespoon Parsley
- 1.5 teaspoon Rosemary
- 1 teaspoon Garlic granules
- 1 teaspoon Onion granules
- ½ teaspoon Black pepper or to taste
- 1 tablespoon Brown sugar
- 1 tablespoon Soy sauce
- 3 tablespoons Lemon juice or Apple Cider Vinegar
- 2 tablespoons Olive oil or melted butter

Directions:

1. Measure out the paprika, parsley, garlic granules, onion granules, rosemary, thyme, oregano, brown sugar, soy sauce, olive oil, lemon juice, and black pepper.
2. Add all the ingredients into a bowl and mix it till well combined.
3. It's ready to apply on Turkey.

Nutritional Value (Amount per Serving):

Calories: 343; Fat: 29; Carb: 21; Protein: 4

Easy Garlic Butter Sauce

Prep Time: 3 Mins
Cook Time: 2 Mins
Serves: 6

Ingredients:

- 110 g Butter slightly salted
- 4 cloves Garlic minced or chopped
- ½ teaspoon Black pepper
- ½ tablespoon Parsley Optional
- ¼ teaspoon Salt If using unsalted butter

Directions:

1. Peel the garlic, rinse and mince, chop or blend.
2. Put a pan on the stove and add in the butter. When it starts to melt, add in the garlic and stir till garlic is fragrant.
3. This takes about 1-2 minutes. Do not cook longer than this to prevent it from burning.
4. Add in the pepper, and herbs if using and stir till combined.
5. Take it off heat and it's ready to use.
6. You can make this sauce in the microwave by simply adding all the ingredients to a microwave-safe bowl, mix till combined, and heat in the microwave for 30 seconds adding by 10 seconds if more time needed till it's melted.

Nutritional Value (Amount per Serving):

Calories: 135; Fat: 15; Carb: 1; Protein: 1

Homemade Bbq Sauce

Prep Time: 5 Mins
Cook Time: 5 Mins
Serves: 2

Ingredients:

- 2 cups Ketchup
- ⅓ cup Apple Cider vinegar
- ⅔ cup Brown sugar
- 2 tablespoon Honey
- 2 tablespoon Smoked Paprika
- 1.5 tablespoon Cayenne pepper or to taste
- 2.5 tablespoon Worcester sauce
- 1 teaspoon Black pepper or to taste
- 1 tablespoon Garlic powder
- ½ cup Water
- 1 teaspoon Mustard powder

Directions:

1. Measure out the ingredients.
2. Place pot on stove then pour in the ketchup.
3. Add apple cider vinegar and all other ingredients.
4. Stir and simmer on low heat for about 5 - 8 minutes or till thickened.
5. Take off heat and leave to cool. Store or use immediately.

Nutritional Value (Amount per Serving):

Calories: 689; Fat: 2; Carb: 166; Protein: 6

Homemade Curry Powder

Prep Time: 5 Mins
Cook Time: 1 Min
Serves: 12

Ingredients:

- 2 tbsp Turmeric
- 2.5 tbsp Ground Coriander
- 2.5 tbsp Cumin
- 1 tbsp Cinnamon
- 1.5 tbsp Ginger
- 1 tbsp Fenugreek
- 1 tbsp Cayenne Pepper
- 1 tspn Black Pepper

Directions:

1. Add all the ingredients in a bowl.
2. Mix thoroughly till well combined.
3. Pour in spice jar or airtight container. Label and store in a cool dry place.

Nutritional Value (Amount per Serving):

Calories: 18; Fat: 0.5; Carb: 3.43; Protein: 0.74

CONCLUSION

In conclusion, air frying is a convenient and healthy cooking method that is becoming increasingly popular in the UK. By using hot air and a small amount of oil, air fryers can cook a wide variety of foods, from chicken and fish to vegetables and even desserts. Air frying offers several potential health benefits, including reduced fat and calorie content, less exposure to harmful compounds, and easier preparation of healthier meals at home. To ensure air frying success, it's important to follow key tips such as preheating the air fryer, not overcrowding the basket, using the right temperature and cooking time, and cleaning the air fryer regularly. Whether you're a seasoned home cook or a novice in the kitchen, an air fryer can be a useful tool for making quick, healthy, and delicious meals.

APPENDIX RECIPE INDEX

A

Aberdeen Angus Burgers 91

Air Fried Beef Sausage Rolls 13

Air Fried Crispy Nugget Caprese 55

Air Fry Banana In Syrup And Nutella ... 76

Air Fryer 10 Minutes Smartie Cookies .. 66

Air Fryer Aubergine 31

Air Fryer BBQ Chicken Breast 49

Air Fryer Brownies 67

Air Fryer Canned Potatoes 27

Air Fryer Chicken Tikka 53

Air Fryer Chicken Wings 48

Air Fryer Corn On The Cob 24

Air Fryer Corned Beef Pasty 59

Air Fryer Doughnuts 72

Air Fryer Doughnuts From Scratch 70

Air Fryer Eggplant 23

Air Fryer Empanadas 18

Air Fryer Fat Rascals 63

Air Fryer Fish Chips 95

Air Fryer Frozen Chicken Nuggets 96

Air Fryer Frozen Tempura Shrimp 87

Air Fryer Frozen Whole Chicken 47

Air Fryer Giant Doughnut Cake 64

Air Fryer Mcchicken Sandwich 81

Air Fryer Onions 30

Air Fryer Parsnip Fries 24

Air Fryer Peeps Rolls 16

Air Fryer Pizza Scrolls 14

Air Fryer Pop Tarts 74

Air Fryer Pork Chops 36

Air Fryer Pork Roast 41

Air Fryer Potatoes And Sausage 94

Air Fryer Prawn Paste Chicken Wings ... 52

Air Fryer Sausages 34

Air Fryer Sliced Potatoes 32

Air Fryer Spinach Fritters 61

Air Fryer Steak Bites 42

Air Fryer Sweet Potato Cubes 29

Air Fryer Thai Meatballs 40

Air Fryer Vegan Fried Rice With Quorn Vegan Fillets 17

Air Fryer Veggie Burgers 21

Air Fryer Yorkshire Pudding Wrap 84

Air-Fried Chicken 51

Air-Fried Chicken Parmesan 54

Air-Fryer Aubergine, Feta And Mushroom Roast 86

Apple Pie Bombs Baked In An Air 77

B

Bacon Wrapped Dates Air Fryer 20

Best Turkey Marinade 99

Bombay Potato Keema Pie 38

Bread Machine Doughnuts Dough 68

C

Chicken And Lamb Chop Karaage In An Air Fryer 44

Chicken Parmigiana Bake 50

Corn Ribs Air Fryer 15

Courgette Fritters 58

Creamy Vegan Tahini Salad Dressing ...98

Crispy Air Fryer Bacon 37

Crispy Air Fryer Cauliflower 12

E

Easy Air Fryer Baked Sweet Potatoes ...28

Easy Garlic Butter Sauce 100

F

Fried Chicken Marinated In The Vietnamese Maggi Soy Sauce 46

Fried Oranges 19

H

Healthier Peanut Butter Cookies With Air Fryer 78

Homemade Bbq Sauce 101

Homemade Curry Powder 102

L

Lime Drizzle Loaf 69

Loaded Potato Skins With Garlic And Sour Cream Dip 87

M

Methi Pakoda With Air Fryer 90

My Air Fryer Honey Mustard Pork Balls 43

My Baked Jacket Potato With Coronation Chicken 93

My Battered Fish Finger Sandwich 80

N

Ninja Foodi Roast Potatoes 89

P

Pulled Aubergine And Chickpea Curry...25

Pumpkin Loaf Cake 75

Q

Quick Simple Air Fryer Fruit Crumble 65

Quorn Korean Crunchy Fillet Sandwich 82

S

Sandwich 83

Spanish Omelette Using Air Fryer 57

Spicy Country Fries 35

T

The Ultimate Air Fryer Pumpkin 71

V

Vegetarian Air Fryer Kimchi Bun 60

Printed in Great Britain
by Amazon